Acknowledgements

When I walked out of prison, I walked into a life full of uncertainty. Mom was sick; Dad and Kevin were still locked up. With plenty to worry about, it never occurred to me that my felonies would have such an impact on what I could do for work. Close to fifteen years later, I remain in fitness because being a former convict limits what I can do, even now.

I'd like to acknowledge first and foremost everyone and anyone who suspended judgment of me until after they knew me. The ones who preferred to look at what I am now, rather than prejudge me for what I was then. If this is you, from the bottom of my heart, thank you.

I'd like to thank my mother, for whom this book is dedicated. If it wasn't for her, I'd have no idea how to look upon where I've been and what I've done with a sense of humor. She always preferred to look forward and laugh, than look back and cry.

And to Rachel, if it wasn't for your vigilance, the following pages would never have been written…

The Fall

In 1990, my father decided to buy diamonds. He plunged into the trade with his partner Bill when they entrusted a local jeweler with their life savings. This foray into his love for shiny, pretty things would prove to be disastrous.

At that time most diamonds flowed through DeBeers, regardless of where they were mined, due to their monopoly on the market. Diamonds were bought and sold in "lots." Most lots yielded a mix of stones ranging from poor to high quality. DeBeers treated their good customers preferentially, bestowing choice lots on them. Otherwise, buying was a gamble, and the house usually won. Dad and Bill never found out what they lost to the dealer, though, because the duplicitous jeweler stole them, shitty and all.

Dad and Billy wanted the hard plastic Samsonite that Billy assured us contained enough diamonds to cover their combined losses. The opportunity to help Dad was presented to my brother, Kevin, first. Being made of the same genetic material that created my father's six foot four, two hundred and thirty pound frame, Kev embodied not only the tools, but fearlessness reserved for daredevils and stuntmen. I was employed to assist Kev only after he conceded that subduing the victim and getting the case was too much, even for him.

I don't remember being shocked, outraged, or even afraid. I said yes without forethought. Kev was onboard; his loyalty to Dad was unwavering. I said yes, in part, because I always wanted to be included in their bond. Besides, we were both addicted to smoking cocaine, so any additional cash would help pay off the growing debt with our dealer.

Listening to Dad plan was surreal. For Kev and me, it was a chance to see Dad shed his cool, calm, and collected demeanor. He dispelled our doubts and fears and cloaked them under a banner of justice. He had been wronged, and our victim deserved what was coming. We were coming.

The plan seemed simple, but there were eventualities impossible to plan for. Sure, we knew where to hide—behind the garage, separate from the house. We knew what to wear—neutral colors, not so dark that we'd stand out against the garage's stark white paint. But neither of us knew how to wait. Do we stand? Sit? Lay? Before we left, Dad reiterated his one and only rule, "If it looks like it's not going to happen, I want you both to high tail it out of there."

Once we were safely behind the garage, I crouched, distorting my frame like a ninja to avoid arousing the suspicion of neighbors. Kev acted nonchalant, as if it were perfectly normal to be standing in the freezing cold behind a garage. Dad waited for us in a stolen car, bathed in the shadows of the trees lining Rte 9 in southern Massachusetts.

"Are we crazy?" I asked.

"SHHHHH!" Kev responded, "He ripped Dad off, remember?"

"Right." I whispered, too softly for him to hear.

Our victim pulled in. His car slithered past, like the snake we both envisioned him to be. Kev pulled me so close, his breath cast moisture on my ear, and whispered, "Count to ten, come out, grab the case, and run." He was gone in a blink.

I counted slowly, anxiously: one-one thousand, two-one thousand, three-one thousand, four-one thousand, then followed. Kevin intercepted our target as he exited his car and started pummeling him. I tried to wrestle the briefcase away from the jeweler, but couldn't pry it from his iron grip, so I stood back while Kev convinced him to let go. As I waited, indoor lights sprang to life in succession, growing closer to the door directly behind me. I furiously jostled the case free from his grasp and took off with Kev in tow.

We darted across the deserted highway, leapt into the car, and sped off with the Samsonite secured by my side. As we drove, Dad said "I just want you boys to know that I don't care what's in that case; I love you both very much."

The case had two combination locks on each latch, each one foolishly left unlocked. I opened the lid, revealing dozens of white paper folds. A fold contains up to thirty diamonds of varying quality and carat weight. Overwhelmed, I couldn't begin to quantify the contents, but I felt like a Pharaoh with a pyramid made of diamonds.

Kev and I woke the next day to find Dad cataloging diamonds into a notebook. Kev demanded cash, a thousand each. Dad didn't argue. We sped off to meet our dealer and blow the remainder on Christmas presents.

Billy later found out our victim claimed the retail value of the loss to his insurance company---one million and change. Fencing, or selling stolen goods, is a bit like accepting your lottery earnings in one lump sum—you only keep a small percentage of your gains. Over the next few months, Billy discretely sold the bulk of the diamonds to a jeweler in south Boston for two hundred thousand. Dad squirreled away the remainder in a safe for a rainy day.

Dodging Murder One

Billy and Dad met in a bar years prior, where they discovered each other's affinity for jewelry. Initially, Billy sold Dad engagement rings and other baubles for our family. In my late teens, Dad became a more frequent customer; he started selling jewelry to supplement the income he earned as computer test equipment salesman. Billy was his supplier. New England was Billy's territory—he knew everyone who was anyone in "the business." This knowledge made him an essential player in the robberies. Sometimes, we thought Billy was our psychic medium.

Billy unearthed information based on a lifetime of connections, like a felony consultant. Dad based his scheming on Billy's obscure recommendations. Together, they concocted a plan to perform a second robbery while Kev and I were home for spring break. They spun a tale that cast us as magnanimous outlaws, above reproach. Supposedly Billy knew a group of "investors" that had been ripped off by an indiscriminating thief. They sought reprisal and felt that fifty thousand dollars from the safe of The Jewel Mart was adequate repayment. The story was crazy and implausible, but Kev and I, fueled more by addiction and greed than conscience, needed little persuading.

We cased the store for weeks before devising our strategy. Casing is acutely boring; it's a slow, grueling observation of minute day-to-day operations, a method of formulating the criminal's business plan. My brother dozed while Dad concentrated on the store. I paid attention to the traffic, ostensibly keeping an eye out for cops, but my mind wandered as I watched the crows pecking at discarded food near a dumpster or eyed a hot red Corvette driving by. Eventually, I realized casing a place before a job was little more than acclimation to the area, becoming part of the backdrop, blending in.

Kev and I didn't know what to do with the detailed information that Dad jotted in his crisp black and white notebook, but we did discover that we were stalking armed prey. We aired our grievances about being shot, but Dad quelled our concerns. His reconnaissance revealed that the owner stowed the gun away just before the store opened. The night before, Dad went over the plan again: we would pose as customers, subdue and handcuff the owner, and clean the place out. Simple as that. "Don't forget to fasten the cuffs nice and tight, and anchor him to the thickest thing you can find. The last thing we need is him getting free."

"Who's going to get his gun?" I asked, terrified Dad would bestow the task on me.

"Once you two have him down and cuffed, I'll find the gun." He turned his attention to Kev. "By the way, how are you going to get him down?"

Kev shrugged.

"I hoped you'd given it more thought than that, son."

"I'll just take him out." Kev sounded offended.

"With all due respect, you don't have the strongest punch in the world," I interjected. "You can throw him a hundred feet, but you don't know how to put any force behind your punch." Kev was strong but lacked the ability to channel his strength from his core and out through his limbs.

"Maybe you'd like me to practice on you?" my brother suggested.

"Quick, get a banana, Dad. Kong is angry."

"Alright, alright, that's fine. If you say you'll get him down, then I'm alright with that. Are you?" Dad asked me in a tone that made me want to liquefy and drizzle into the heating vent next to my right foot.

"I'm fine. I'm just worried because there are guns involved."

"I agree, Dad," my brother said. "This is nuts. What if he starts shooting?"

"Don't worry. I'll have my .22, and trust me, I'll get to it before he can get to his if he is that stupid. Just stick to the plan. Get him cuffed and out of sight, and I'll take care of the safe. Your brother will clear out the cases." The hair on the back of my neck stood at his casual tone, the nonchalant way he talked about us taking on a guy with a gun, otherwise meek or not. "We'll be in and out of there in fifteen minutes."

The next morning, I heard Dad leave for the gym. "Did you sleep at all?" I called out.

"No," Kev replied from his room, although I heard him snoring around three.

"Ready to do this?" he asked.

"Yeah," I answered. "Are you sure those cuffs work?"

"I'm sure," he said. Then, after a moment of silence, I asked, "Are we bad people?"

It was the first moral question posed since we started. Bad is as bad does — I knew that deep down. Kev just reiterated what Dad told us a few short hours before: "We'll be fine. In and out in fifteen minutes."

Dad analyzed our intelligence and surmised that mid-morning was the best time to execute. Dad was armed; Kev and I had gloves and handcuffs decorated with pink frilly lace, like all serious criminals.

At exactly 10:30am we walked into Jewel Mart, but for reasons unknown to us, the owner had decided to remain armed that day. Instinctively, we all knew that continuing our plan could lead to gunfire and disaster. But we were right in the middle of executing the plan. We gained entry. The owner buzzed us in after

Dad spoke through the intercom. "My son here is getting married. We'd like to see some wedding bands."

Once inside, I flanked Kev's left. Dad took a position on his right. Kev's only obstacles were the cases. Inside, jewelry glittered under carefully placed track lights. Dad's noncommittal to anything presented prompted the owner to suggest he look out back. Out of earshot, I huffed, "Are you trying to give me a fucking heart attack?"

"Fuck off." Kev snapped while looking at Dad, "What should I do?"

Dad took stock of our surroundings. Although we cased the place for weeks, an unchecked variable presented itself, something we hadn't planned for. The gun turned the tides in favor of our victim. He held a trump card we thought was still in the deck. We walked away reluctantly, yet prudently.

A week later, the owner of the Jewel Mart was robbed by another enterprising criminal and was lethally wounded during exchange of gunfire. Eyewitnesses described a car speeding away from the scene, prompting surveillance of the vehicle owner's home. Soon, officers hidden outside watched the crook crawl out a bathroom window, then stash the murder weapon and stolen jewelry under a neighbor's porch. The story made national headlines.

Nothing about that fatal incident revealed to us the insanity of what we were doing. Dad praised his own uncanny instincts, as if his knack for walking away unscathed came from an innate sixth sense, rather than dumb luck. He viewed us as the Teflon coated, robbing hoods. Kev and I returned to school while our narcissistic father worked with Billy to find another target.

Burlington

We were both on the fast track to failing out of school. With unlimited funds, classes played second fiddle to partying. But even our insatiable appetite for damaging brain cells couldn't put a dent in the pile. We both bought cars. I bought a Ford Bronco II. Kev a shiny maroon Trans Am I dubbed the death trap because of his propensity to drive up, on, and around anything in his way. Dad secured loans for us both by co-signing and insisted we both work to remain "on the grid." I took a part time job as a cashier at a grocery store. Kev was a doorman at a sleazy bar.

Neither of us was surprised when we came home for summer break to find Dad in the early planning stage of another job since our last yielded nothing, not even the wisdom of hindsight. It was ours (mostly his) uncanny instinct to avoid the pitfalls of perpetrating that lead us to walk away unscathed from the last job. We bought into the notion that we were too smart to get caught.

But Kev and I felt a measure of relief because we were convinced that the plan was too elaborate for our simple trio. We needed to rent a storefront using an alias and cash to avoid creating a paper trail. We'd need a female "employee" to lull our victim into a false sense of security. Finally, we'd also need access to Bob's car since after the murder; salesmen only carried faux jewelry into stores in case they were robbed. We nearly talked Dad out of it, but within a week he rented a store in a strip mall, and convinced his girlfriend, Nancy, to play the part of proprietor. Dad was confident that we wouldn't get caught. Bob was already under suspicion of filling false insurance claims, a fact that would throw the authorities off our trail.

For this job it seemed prudent that we all carry, meaning, we all were armed. The mere suggestion sent torrents of fear through me, but it was hard to argue with the plain as day logic Dad presented, "Three guns are better than one."

As a safety precaution we went to a local firing range so that Dad could school us on the proper use of something that seemed so simple. Point and shoot, what more was there to know? He respected each one of his gun's power, and in turn, nurtured ours. He owned a .357 nickel plated revolver, a .9 millimeter beretta, and his trusty .22. People around us at the range turned to look as he pointedly informed us, "This is not a toy." An impression neither Kev nor I was under. But there were other factoids he regaled us with, like the kickback of a slide action is different from that of a revolver. A hollow point (A pit or hollowed out shape at the tip) causes the bullet to expand upon entering a target in order to decrease penetration and disrupt more tissue as it travels through the target. By the end of the day I was hitting the inner circles of the target with the .357, finding it easier to control than the .9 millimeter. Kev loved the idea of having 16 bullets in the clip and one in the chamber, commenting, "Who needs good aim?"

But there was one more problem I needed to address with Dad and that was Kevin's low blood sugars. If during the job, Kev's sugar plummeted, we'd have a real problem, which is why Dad and I carried glucose tabs. Kev's propensity toward violence when low prompted my concern for all parties involved, since Kev was indiscriminate when delivering blows during a blackout. Dad used Kev's lack of experience with firearms against him when he decided that Kev's would be the only weapon without bullets.

On the day of the job, a haze concealed the sun as morning commuters made their way through an intersection between opposing gas stations that vied for patronage by offering discounted gallons every other Tuesday. I parked my Bronco behind the building as planned. Dad arrived with Kev an few minutes later and we all went inside the store to meet Nancy who had already left Bob a voice message letting him know he could come by anytime. Kev plopped himself on the floor near the door leading to the front. I took a position across from him, the .357 felt like a five pound thorn in my side. The waiting was excruciating.

Eleven thirty eight, over two hours later than expected, Bob called to let Nancy know he was on the way. We perked like hyenas detecting newly spilled blood in the air. We took our positions according to plan: Dad by the door, Nancy behind an empty display case, and Kev and I on other side of the wall leading into the back.

"Good morning, Bob." I heard Nancy say.

"Hi, sorry I'm late." Bob replied. I tried to ascertain from his voice his threat level. Was he hulking, menacing, or meek? Billy described him as soft and completely unthreatening, but nothing in his voice helped me determine either way.

Kev plastered himself against the wall holding the .9 millimeter in his upturned arm, keeping it flush against the wall. I did the same except my gun remained in my waistband.

Nancy said, "Why don't we head out back and talk, they're measuring for carpets out here and I'm sure we'll just be in the way." And with that, Bob was delivered to us after Dad gave him a shove through the door.

Kev immediately directed him my way with such force, Bob's body nearly toppled the wall dividing the store, front to back. I feverishly searched his body for his gun, finding it in his back pocket, holstered. I tossed it aside as Kev led Bob to a wooden chair in the corner.

"Keep your eyes shut." Kev demanded of Bob.

I began taping Bob's listless frame to the chair beginning with his feet and working my way up.

Dad joined us just as I had placed a six inch length of tape over Bob's eyes. Once he was secure, Dad questioned him.

"The sooner we get what we came for, the sooner you go home, got it?" Dad asked. Bob nodded. "Good, now walk me through this alarm system, what keys disarm it?"

"They're on a separate ring attached to the larger, three master keys and a tubular. The tubular disarms the alarm. The masters get you past the other locks." Bob's voice was uneven, shaky.

"Good. Now sit tight and we'll be on our way soon." Dad assured him after handing me the keys.

I tried to move inconspicuously. Sweat coated my skin. I stood between two parked cars. The one behind me might've been blue, or maybe black. It was tough to tell in the reflection of the car that captured my attention. Of the three keyholes on the back quarter panel of the maroon sedan in front of me, only one opened the trunk. The other two tripped the alarm. Dad remained watchful in front of the store.

Dad's presence eased my anxiety, but only slightly. In those seconds that I stared at the three possible keyholes, those seconds allotted by both my own panic and the gravity of the situation, I was acutely aware of certain aspects of my surroundings. For one, I knew that a man approached Dad, the proprietor from next door sauntering by, summoned by his curiosity about a new neighbor. I also knew there was a cop car nearby, and the black and white of the vehicle re-ignited the frenzy of panic inside. The cop pulled into a space just as I inserted the key. I waited to turn it, looking to Dad for guidance, but his flaring eyes incited even more panic rather than relieve it with some calm parental guidance. He ducked into the store to warn Kev, and his abandonment of his post, of me, struck a nerve, the feeling both new and ancient, as old as I was anyway.

The officer exited the cruiser. I looked away, toward the sign that says six cents off every other Tuesday. I found myself wishing it was Tuesday and that I was a commuter anxious only that I might be late for work, wishing I was anyone but me. The cop entered the drugstore. I unclenched and turned the key. The trunk popped open. I wondered why everyone around me didn't stop and look at me.

When Dad was back at his post, I nodded in his direction. The trunk only opened halfway; a thick padlocked chain prevented it from opening further. I fished through the key ring to find the one etched "Master." Crouching to reach inside, I slid the key into the lock and sent it crashing to the floor of the trunk. Metal against metal echoed through the parking lot as each link of the chain rubbed against the hinges.

Dad stood behind me. Inside the trunk, the chain lay limp, conforming to the shape of the suitcases. I rose as Dad surveyed the contents of the trunk: six large suitcases, one duffle bag, and two trash bags.

"Let's get it out back and loaded into the truck," he whispered.

With two of the cases and Dad in tow, we passed Kev holding his gun on our blindfolded hostage. Behind the building, we loaded the cases into my Bronco. "Let's get the rest and get out of here." Dad continued to speak under his breath, which seemed a pointless exercise in being discrete, I found it maddening.

Kev's eyes followed us as we slithered back through the store. Dad grabbed the final two cases while I cleared out the duffle bag and the two trash bags.

"Leave the trash." Dad snapped over his shoulder. I ignored him.

Once everything was loaded, we returned to get Kev. Dad bent forward, retrieved our hostage's wallet, and removed the license. "We know where you live now. I had better read in tomorrow's paper that you were robbed by three black men, understand?"

Our captive nodded. Kev cocked the hammer. "Please don't kill me," the man begged with a shudder.

"No one's going to kill you," Dad replied. "When we're gone, count to five hundred." Dad turned and waved me off — time to get out of there.

The morning traffic gone, I drove away quickly, and with the strip mall in my rearview, I breathed deeply for the first time in hours. In spite of little traffic, the drive was excruciatingly slow. When I finally got home, I rid the house of natural light and poured a glass of wine, forcing it down my sandpaper throat. The burps were part gas relief and part wretch. The two hemispheres of my brain waged a war against one another. The left wanted me to sit, but the right needed me to move. The left wanted me to lie still, but the right needed me to pace. The left wanted me to binge, but the right needed me to purge.

When Dad and Kev finally arrived, we removed the cases from the truck, stacked them in the kitchen, and began the process of dissecting the loot.

"I told you not to take those trash bags. Get rid of them," Dad barked.

I heaved one onto the couch, tore the plastic apart, and revealed manila envelopes filled with invoices. Dad peered over my shoulder.

"Friggin' receipts! Now there's evidence lying around that we don't need." His words stung. Kev nodded in agreement with him.

I built a fire and fished through the bags. I took a gander at random invoices and cringed at the amounts we'd get pennies on the dollar for, but the third envelope looked like an Andrew Jackson clone convention — it was full of twenties. "Oh father, might I confer with you briefly?" I remarked in my best faux English accent.

As he walked toward me, a fistful of gold chains dangled from his hand. His expression suggests he expected to find me in a cloud of smoke after forgetting to open the flue. I dumped the cash on the coffee table and watched the corners of his mouth stretch from ear to ear. The calories Kev gnawed on drizzled down his chin and spilled out of his dropped jaw.

As Dad counted, the fire engulfed more invoices. I discovered three more envelops full of cash, ten grand and change all together. Kev scooped up three piles of bills from the table and said, "We're out of here."

Dad stopped inventorying long enough to ask, "Three grand? Where are you going?"

"We're taking off. We need to blow off some steam, maybe go shopping," Kev replied. I was thinking about the fact that he was a man of few words, that he only knows a few words.

Kev and I rented the most expensive suite in the swankiest hotel we could find. Then Kev called our dealer, who delivered. I flipped through TV stations, watching everything and nothing at all. Several lines of white powder vanished from the bedside table. Finally, I mustered the strength to ask what had been on my mind since the robbery.

Turning to Kev, who sat at the desk tinkering with his pile of white powder, I asked, "Do you feel bad for him?"

After a short pause, he nodded in affirmation.

Dad never asked why we always came home broke and nimbus-cloud pale. On this occasion, he was preoccupied with making a place to hide our stash. After the first job, while we were waiting for Billy to show to help tally the score, I proposed we squirrel away some of the loot so we didn't spend every dime as we heisted it. Apparently Dad was listening better than I thought because he selected a few choice pieces to put away that Billy wouldn't know about, that Dad could sell on his own.

"I could use a hand, son," Dad yelled from the bottom stair.

Kev made a beeline to his room. I walked downstairs and positioned myself by his side. Dad knelt. The Sawzall hissed, sparks flew in all directions. The smell of burnt concrete filled the basement. Shrapnel hit my bare legs.

"Now what?" I asked as we both stared down at a hundred pound block of concrete.

"Hand me that chisel and hammer and I'll show you," Dad replied.

He centered the chisel and swung. Sparks scattered off the otherwise unaffected block. He swung again, and the block succumbed, splitting into three uneven chunks. Dad handed them off, and I carried them outside to fill in the half-finished granite walkway leading from the back porch to the driveway. Dad pulled shovelfuls of dirt out of the hole, and I dumped those too.

Dad sunk the safe inside and filled the hole with fresh concrete, smoothing it once there was enough. The wet concrete sucked the safe in. Set to his liking, Dad placed our nest egg inside: one packet of diamonds, three tennis bracelets, money envelopes, and a velvet roll of variables taken from the Burlington job.

The money flowed in quickly in the coming months, and the safe downstairs filled completely. I paid off my Ford Bronco II, installed a car phone, and jazzed the stereo with four amps and a base tube.

Summer came on the coattails of Kev's umpteenth DUI. This time, he tried to outrun the cops and they slapped him with habitual offender status for his efforts, which carried a mandatory year in jail.

"No son of mine is going to jail," Dad said resolutely. So, in lieu of jail, Kev sped off to Clearwater, Florida in a metallic maroon Trans Am bought at cost from our dealer, who used the car dealership to justify his grandiose income.

Kev always controlled the drugs. When he doled out the amounts, my share was always smaller. When there was only a little left, he'd send me to bed. It made me so mad that when he left for Florida, my daily habit skyrocketed.

Brainwashing

Objects in motion remain in motion unless external forces are applied. It's a law of physics but also of life. When my confession interrupted Dad's weekend work schedule he asked, "What are you addicted to?"

"Coke," I answered.

He sighed. "What do you want to do about it?"

"I need rehab."

"I can't afford rehab."

"I don't know what else to do," I responded, stung by the idea that the safe full of cash and stolen goods never crossed his mind.

"I have no experience with this, son." It was his patented response.

"How can you say that after being married to Mom for ten years?"

"I guess I can't understand how someone can't just stop. I smoked cigarettes, and then I stopped. I didn't need rehab or therapy. I just quit."

"Can you just come pick me up?"

When he picked me up, we sped down the highway with nothing but a chasm of silence between us and an admission whose validity was only measurable in the minutes after, when there was no time to reconsider, the way I reconsidered by the time we reached home.

Withdrawal came on quick, and I slept off the worst of it. Dad came in and sat on the bed.

"There's a bus leaving from Manchester in a few hours that will take you right back to campus." His weight collapsed the edge of the mattress. "I'm going to take away your truck. That way you can concentrate on school. It's too late in the semester to drop out. I'd hate to see all the tuition money go to waste. I'll pay the rent and send you just enough money for food. Beyond that, no cash," he said, and then he hugged me.

While I was in the shower, I scoffed at his idea. School was the worst place to send me, but it was too late for debates. I already decided that I'd use again and again to spite him.

Neighborhoods whizzed by. I read billboards from the last seat of the Greyhound Dad so effortlessly dropped me off to catch. I plotted the whole trip. Waiting in the mailbox at school was a rent check amongst the eviction notices and inquiries from school asking if I dropped out. I forged my landlord's name again and called my dealer.

The irony of lighting a gumball sized hit was that, a few short hours prior, I was willing to go to rehab. Coke filled my lungs. Blood drained from my extremities. My heart raced toward an unmarked goal. I dove for the barrel and threw up nothing, since food was as appealing as sobriety.

Obsession bred compulsion. For three days, I didn't leave the room, not even to pee, making use of an empty bottle under the window sill. I searched the rug for stray bits of coke and ended up smoking nook-and-cranny crumbs from an English muffin. I finally gave up and read *Wiseguy* over and over, cover to cover, finding my perspective had changed. I related on a level few readers could.

Word followed the forged check trail back to Dad, and so he sent Mom to get me at school. Sobriety rounded out the edges etched by her decades of drinking. She was plumper but still outspoken, and she delivered an ultimatum at the end of a long hug. "You have two choices: you can stay here and become homeless, or you can come with me and go to rehab."

"I guess I'll go with you," I replied.

We hugged again. She smelled of Eve Light 120s infused with Silver Fox hair products. Sobriety grayed her too, it seemed. The physical changes complimented the ideological ones: She dumped Catholicism for an earth-based religion, St. John's for a Unitarian church, the city for the outskirts. She packed up and moved to a small New Hampshire town but worried about what the rest of the family might think of her tree-hugging, incense-burning persona, and so she kept it secret. Despite her demons, she was infectiously happy.

Mom let me sleep an entire twenty-four hours to catch up. I woke to a telephone being thrust into my face. "It's a sober house with an open bed. They want to talk to you." Mom left no room for discussion.

"Hi there. My name is Phil, and I'm the intake director at Keystone Hall. Your mother tells me you're interested in seeking help for your addiction." The several packs a day rasp in his voice grated on my last nerve. "Yeah, I guess," was all I mustered.

"Well, we're not a treatment center necessarily, but we can give you a safe place to hang while we find you a bed somewhere else," he said, ending with directions for how to get there.

Mom was ecstatic.

Keystone Hall was a daycare for degenerates, so I fit right in. Carl searched my belongings for drugs, paraphernalia, and weapons. I joked that, if I had any drugs, I would have been elsewhere. Carl smirked but wasn't amused. Nurse Ratchet, as I came to call her, took my vitals and asked if I was suicidal. I told her, "No, but the day is young," for which I was put on fifteen minute suicide watch. Carl became my new hemorrhoid, but he didn't have to look very far for me because I never left my room.

Phil strongly suggested I attend a group session. I did, sitting in the back and listening but not taking part.

"Adult children of alcoholics become numb as a way of coping." He cued the group to comment, then prodded us with his eyes. Someone chimed up. It wasn't me.

A bed opened at The Farnam Center. Thirty days of intense treatment, moldy bread, and questions, lots of questions. "Why do you want to know about my father, lady?" I asked the intake counselor when silence failed to telegraph my intent to skate through the next thirty days unnoticed.

She yammered about catharsis. Yada this, yada that. All I could think about was soup ladles after hearing some kid in the waiting room talk about how he cooked up half ounces of cocaine in soup ladles. I couldn't wait to fill a ladle coke.

Dad and Kev visited. Kev wore a brand new shiny rope chain, indicating they pulled off the Harwich, Rhode Island job without me. My expendability stung. "Don't worry. We've decided to give you a cut," Dad whispered with a wink.

Kev gave me the details near the coffeemaker while we waited for a fresh pot: "We waited at this guy's house. Dad sat in his car and waited while I sat at a stop sign down the street. Dad pulled in behind him, and I backed up, boxing him in. Dad unloaded the trunk while I kept an eye on the guy." Kev's breath reeked of weed. He sipped coffee while he gave me the rundown. Dad and Kev left after twenty minutes.

Mom showed up shortly thereafter. "Your brother was here?"

"Yeah, they just left."

"That explains the look in your eyes. He didn't bring you anything, did he?" she asked.

"No, Mum. He didn't bring me anything," I replied, unsure why the question offended me.

"Hey, no one knows better than your dear ol' mom what it's like to be here. Hell, there's a wing named after me at Danvers Hospital," she joked, which was entirely plausible because she spent the better part of the seventies there as a patient. "Have you given any more thought to coming to live with me after treatment?"

"And what is there for me to do in Epping, Mom? You live in the sticks," I said, still smarting from her question, her accusation.

"Listen, we both know that being near your brother is bad news, especially if you're serious about staying clean. And you could pull the wool over your father's eyes without even trying, trust me."

I nodded. She pitched some more: "Besides, it'll give us a chance to spend time together. And I could totally use your help with the ducks." Mom awaited the emergence of twelve hatchlings nesting in a cardboard box in the kitchen, warmed by a heating lamp.

"I can't believe you bought duck eggs."

"I'm so excited for them to hatch. Maybe you'll be home to see it happen. I was so glad to sell the old house. I love Epping. It's so quiet and peaceful." Some people's faces light up, and some could even be said to glow; the difference for my mother lay in the duration of the glowing. She glowed for the rest of the visit, especially after I said I'd come home.

Teri, my counselor, called it the first positive move I made since he'd known me, but he offered no advice on duck rearing. In fact, I felt better since my arrival, my head clearer, and I knew for the first time in ages that I really wanted to do what I was about to do.

I walked through a secondhand smoke cloud to get to the pay phones. Dad accepted the collect call and did his best to sound chipper. "Hey there, son. How are you holding up?"

"Fine, Dad. Listen, I think Mom's going to pick me up, and I'm going to live with her for awhile. She begged. You know how she is. So I thought maybe I'd give it a try." The emotion I hoped he'd reciprocate welled inside and cracked my voice.

"Whatever you think is best, son." His tone jumped a decibel higher, proving Dad valued his solace.

The day Mom picked me up, I hurried out of the facility. I hated long goodbyes. I saw Teri before his morning cup of Joe, knowing he was less likely to gush without his morning jolt. He said, "You're only as sick as your secrets, Bryan. Good luck." I was bewildered, wondering how he knew I held back.

Mom offered the second bedroom, but unable to feel at home among Mom's angel figurines and crystals, I chose the futon. I woke every morning to a list of chores, feed the ducks, clean, mow. But there were extras that were quintessentially Mom, like dusting the light bulbs in the bathroom.

I watched the duck hierarchy with amusement. The other ducks weren't allowed to enter the freshly filled kiddie pool until the bull male bathed. Then he allowed one female to enter and submerged her, having his way. My job was to herd them back into the yard when they strayed, and I noted more than once that webbed feet slapping the pavement sounded like babies clapping.

I craved cocaine, and sometimes I found myself reducing every household object to its pawnshop value. Porcelain angels yielded a few dollars at best, so I eyed Mom's most prized possession, her decades old Hummel collection. But the impulse abated when I refocused my energy on more pressing issues, like the ducks harassing the bunnies by lying under their cage and quaking sweet nothings. I broke up their party, and then sat on the porch swing, basking in clarity. I noticed there wasn't a single tree without a bird house.

When Dad invited me to lunch, I knew there was another job in the works. We exchanged pleasantries as the waitress brought Dad his usual house white. I sipped water, the sweat from the glass saturated a bar napkin, and chewed fish saturated in butter. Dad inhaled a salad.

"How is it living with Mom?" he asked.

"Fine," I answered.

"Kev is coming home. You up for some work?" He smiled, revealing two equidistant gold caps, one on each side of his mouth, and I wondered if this was the beginning of an intricate series of cogs and cams and crankshafts that powered the machine before me.

"Sure," I lied, pacifying him. I planned to bow out over the phone later.

He signaled for the check and led me to his car, which was perched on a hill overlooking an ATM. He said, "We need a car for the next job. See that ATM across the parking lot?" I nodded involuntarily. "People get out with the car running. Stand nearby, and when they go inside the ATM, grab the car and drive off. I'll follow you."

I became acutely aware of the ebb and flow of a world outside the minor universe of our nefarious intent. Dad had the instincts of a predator. He was able to see two dimensionally, to see the lapse in time between transactions, when the driver would be unaware a crime was being perpetrated. "Just time it right, son."

My ass suctioned to the seat. The bravado I inherited from my father may be buried deep within my genetic code, but that bravado was not automatic, at least not constant. I knew I couldn't do it.

I was about to confess my inadequacies when a cop car pulled up and parked near the ATM. "Oh, shit. This place is too hot. What if I was about to do it just then?" I said, trying to hide the relief. We called the car heist off, but only at that ATM. Dad and Kev used the same strategy at another ATM with success a week later. All was set for the Littleton job.

Littleton

I succumb to sleep just after Mom leaves for work. Chores scribed on a sticky note will have to wait: ducks, bunnies, lawn, and bathrooms, bulbs included. Images of things gone awry play out until I wipe all thoughts clean save one: What if he fights back?

Sunlight peaks over the horizon as I reach Dad's house. He mills about as Kev swishes OJ around in his mouth, to assuage his cotton mouth, I assume. Dad's briefcase is open on the counter, his .22 holstered inside and the .9 mm placed carefully beside it. We will need both, but I wave off the .357 Dad offers.

"This could be as big as Burlington if Billy is right about this guy." Dad's aim is to put things into perspective so we know what might be gained here in exchange for the risk, but I know Kev translates these assurances that the risk is worth it into more coke and rent in sunny Florida. He tops off a syringe with insulin, NPH, the slower acting.

"No regular?" Dad asks.

"No. I can manage it better without," he replies as I grab a handful of Reese's, just in case.

The parking lot is packed when we pull up. The brick building houses businesses with obscure names like Global Tech and Omni Corp, nothing to indicate what these outfits do for money. Dad waits in an undisclosed location, and Kev and I take refuge in the lobby.

There's no way to tell exactly when our victim will arrive. We only have an approximate time — nine a.m. At eight fifty-five, Kev moves toward the door with me in tow. Get the case and keys, case and keys, case and keys. The simple instructions repeat in my mind like a macabre mantra. A powder blue sedan pulls in. I time each step: left foot — case, right foot — keys.

The inevitable prolonged like the seconds before a collision, our paths finally cross and his eyes glue to the gun Kev sticks in his face. "Give me the case and your keys or I'll blow your fucking head off," Kev threatens. The man acquiesces. I hurry to the car with the case as I fish for the key with the Chrysler symbol.

Dad follows us out of the lot. I watch for our victim to run for the lobby in my peripheral vision. I step on it when I do see him, screeching the tires and fostering Kev's ire. He tells me to slow the fuck down. I find a lot to ditch the car in and scurry out of the vehicle as Dad pulls up. We empty the trunk while Kev gobbles Reese's.

I imagine the list of side effects from this massive adrenaline rush: *Caution! Armed robberies may cause paranoia, palpitations, restlessness, and difficulty breathing. Do not attempt if you have heart problems, weakened immune response, or common sense.*

Facial Recognition

He slides what I think is a copy of the contract, perhaps outlining where and when to relinquish my soul, across the table. He smirks as I unfold the document, commenting on what tickles him so pink. "Billy and I agree that it looks nothing like me. Jeez, you'd think these composite artists would be better at this sort of thing."

I disagree with Dad and Billy's assessment. Not only did the police composite artist nail the deadpan eyes, they captured the essence of a man who schemes as easily as breathes.

"And you think this *doesn't* look like you?" I ask.

"No way. Why? do you?"

"It's a perfect likeness, Dad. This picture looks totally like you."

"Nah, no way. Look at this thing closer. You only think it looks like me because you know the drawing is supposed to be of me." He spreads it out, as if the crinkles distort my perception, and then folds up the paper and tucks it away inside his suit — case closed. "How's school, son?" He asks because I used my enrollment in an Associate's program to avoid the Cape job he and Kev pulled with some new help.

Dad and his girlfriend, Nancy, posed as a married couple looking for an anniversary gift. Billy advised that, if they looked upscale, the clerk would bring out the high-end pieces he knew the store kept locked in the safe. Kev then walked in, scaled the counter, and cuffed the owner. Dad and Nancy cleaned out the store, including the safe.

But Dad is unsatisfied. "It wasn't our best haul, but we did all right. I have a few other things in the works. I figure two or three more jobs like Burlington and we'll be set." His chest swells with excitement.

"What's in the works?" I ask, feeling the same shaky unease as I did when waiting for a half ounce but knowing that sweet numbness would not accompany delivery.

"Your brother is coming up for Christmas. Billy's setting up a few things now. We might get a few done before the holiday."

"Great," is all I say.

On city sidewalks, busy sidewalks, dressed in holiday style, I stand in the foyer of a McDonald's in Boston's financial district, nauseous at the song playing on the sound system amidst the sounds of orders being taken and people shuffling to their seats.

Shoppers spill onto the sidewalks from overflowing stores. Dad and Kev wait for my signal two blocks away in front of Fed-Ex. I am to transmit. *The gravel's on the way* through the walkie-talkie to let them know our target left the Jeweler's Building. For this job, I'm only back-up, and so I hold the walkie-talkie, ready to follow our target after signaling Dad.

He finally passes. "Gravel on the way," I say, and I match his gate, nearly step on his heels before backing off. I picture myself a predator, but in truth I feel like a scavenger, maybe a raven picking through what's left of a happy meal spilled in the street. This guy's arms are loaded with Fed-Ex boxes. One contains Billy's order, which we refer to as risk insurance.

Kev plows toward him like a heat-seeking missile. If he isn't careful, they'll crash instead of nonchalantly crossing paths like Dad suggested.

"Give me the fucking boxes or I'll blow your head off!" His words ricochet off cobble, concrete, and glass. Bystanders glance in his direction. I close in directly behind the man.

"Excuse me?" he asks. Kev socks him as he points the gun into his face. Fed-Ex boxes tumble as the target's body thumps onto the pavement. He squawks, "Hey! Hey!"

Dad swoops in, scoops up boxes, and zips off. Kev bolts. My knee jerk reaction is to offer the man a hand up. He accepts, grasping his jaw. "Thanks," he says. By then, others gather, allowing me to blend in with the crowd and fade away. I meet Dad and Kev at the car. They sit inside waiting. The boxes are secure in the trunk.

Unloading, I notice no variance from box to box. What's worse, something heavy shifts in each one. When Dad pulls a thick book from a box, we realize all seven contain catalogs.

Billy explained to Dad later that the jeweler called to say his package would be a day late. The jeweler apparently picked up our walkie-talkie transmissions on his police scanner. He found the cryptic nonsense about gravel suspicious enough to hold off a day on sending out the real goods. Dad is livid at our failure and goes right to work planning another job.

Evolution is harsh on those who misuse the power of adrenaline for anything other than ducking fast moving trains or mortal threats. In the past, I'd guzzle booze or smoke coke to counter the effects. Left unchecked, the adrenaline makes my skin crawl, and so I live vicariously through Kev, driving him to meet his dealer. "Spend enough time in a barber shop, and you're bound to get a haircut," said George, my sponsor. His warning echoes in my head, and so I drop Kev off and get my ass to an AA meeting.

On the first day of class, amidst a barrage of complaints about the syllabus, the professor, Marcel, stands on his desk and orders everyone to take out a piece of paper. "Write your name and a grade and pass it forward." He is a former preacher turned professor, and he is responding to the concerns of the class, most of which sound like nitpicking to me.

Once he has all the papers, he asks, "Can I teach now?" But his point doesn't have the intended effect. Through the murmurs and guffaws, I think, "This man is either a genius, an idiot, or some strange combination of both."

The curriculum calls for all students to be placed in internships at area hospitals and rehabs. Placement is based on what Marcel thinks of each student's progress. I'm given a contact name at a rehab not far from Dad's house, and this rehab program is where I meet the adult chemical dependency unit director, Mark, for the first time.

He nonchalantly saunters into his office where I am waiting and shakes my hand. His tailored double-breasted sport coat is unbuttoned and flaps with the energy of his overcompensating strides, the sure walk of a man with a Napoleon Complex. His mannerisms are meant to let me know that he is the cock of this particular walk. "I want you to help people, but we still gotta pay the fuckin' the bills. Know what I mean?" His tone indicates he means this only partly in jest.

I soon figure out that the silver spoon that pacified him early on was later melted down and molded into a frame for his Harvard MBA. Mark walks with ILS, Invisible Lat Syndrome, which means he holds his arms at a forty degree angle to his body and pushes out his chest as if he were a weight lifter with more meat on his bones than a gorilla; and he acts like everything he says holds the wisdom of his vast experience.

He tells me to shadow Patti, a unit counselor. I walk in on her phoning in a prescription for Zanax. "Panic attacks," she says after hanging up. "We'll keep this between you and me?"

"Of course," I say, feeling my face flush.

She stands to walk out, stopping briefly to pick up a file folder. "We're late for Feelings Group. Ever been?"

"Not since rehab," I say, letting her know I have firsthand experience.

She snickers. "Better clam up then. They'll eat you alive if they know you're green."

Nurses zip around behind the front desk like worker bees, and I note that counselors stay out of their flight path lest they feel the sting of nursely sarcasm. I give the desk a wide berth, but Patti skims the edge, tapping the desk with her knuckle.

The Feelings Group session is held in the TV room. The chairs are rearranged in a circle. I loosen my tie to make way for the knot forming in my throat. The two remaining empty chairs oppose each other, coincidentally or by design I do not know. The others are filled with patients of varying sobriety. New fish are the easiest to pinpoint, reddened in areas coinciding with their particular poison.

Patti props her chin on two extended fingers, as mine is the only presence under scrutiny by the others. She nods to the petite blond on my right, who reads the rules from a laminated card. "If the door is closed, you can't come in. Speak in 'I' statements only — do not project. Rescuing, offering tissues, empathy, or sympathy are strictly prohibited." The room falls silent after she finishes.

Patti's confidence is in her blank stare. I follow her gaze to a poster filled margin to margin with emotions. Then around the room her eyes go and mine follow, stopping at each nametag and assigning one of those emotions: starting with Cheryl — happy, Nick — tired, Ed — ahh-ahh-annoyed, Margaret — worried, Sam — pissed, Patti — optimistic. Then her eyes come to me and I associate a word, an emotion, with myself — hopeful.

Nick asks, "Who's the new guy?"

Patti replies, "A new counseling intern."

Nick smirks. "Jesus, another one?"

Cheryl chimes in, "What school do you go to?"

Patti interrupts, "Cheryl please."

Cheryl apologizes.

Silence…

Nick explodes, "This place sucks!"

Patti, perfectly calm, replies, "Did you want to phrase that so that we can identify how you feel?"

Nick pushes. "Yes, Patti, I would. This-place-fucking-sucks!"

Patti asks, "Can you pick an emotion from the wall and let us know what you're feeling?"

Nick escalates his attack. "Well, jeez. I guess I'm angry. I would bet that even fresh face over here could figure that out." He is waving his thumb my way. I hope that no one notices me shrink.

Patti adds, "And this is an ongoing issue. What have you learned from previous outbursts?"

Nick's pause mutes Patti, who stares blankly again, as if away from a chess board so as not to telegraph her next move. The truth is, I realize, she knows not only Nick's next move but his next five.

Nick deflates. "That such outbursts indicate that I am impulsive."

Patti owns him now. "And why is that of concern to you?"

Nick bends her way. "Because, when I'm impulsive, I use."

After the group adjourns, after many a sob and many a whine and many a calm rejoinder from Patti, she says, "Toughest group you'll run here. Some mornings I dread it, especially with that ticking time bomb, Nick, here."

A week later, in a pinch to find coverage, Mark offers me a permanent position as a mental health counselor right around the same time Dad offers me a position as lookout on the next job.

He plans jobs feverishly, one after another, setting the cap on when we will have enough higher and higher: one mil, two mil, then five. He rents an office suite while Nancy buffers the next victim with promises of purchasing his entire inventory. Kev flies home. I bow out because of midterms.

They rob Jacob, our very first victim, again because Dad has an itch for the guy. So much of an itch that just as Dad is leaving the scene, he gets an inkling that things went a little too smoothly. Jacob's calmness prompts Dad to go back and pat him down, and under his dress shirt is a holster full of loose diamonds.

Dad likens the score to Burlington in terms of the haul, but he reneges on his promise that this job is the last one. "Billy says there's a guy in Weymouth that keeps over twenty grand in his safe for pawns. It could be a big job. We sure could use you on this," he tells me on the phone.

On the ride to our meeting, I am resolute that I will not do another job; but as always, when he starts talking, I buckle in front of him. But I notice that the Weymouth job lacks all of our usual panache. There is no elaborate set up, no duck tape, no splitting up. Just a store, just the cuffs, and we all travel to and from the job in the same car.

We drive to a store just off a main street in Weymouth, and Dad and Kev enter while I stand outside, armed with a squeegee and bucket of soapy water. I wash the windows. Dad and Kev subdue the owner and clean out the store, and then Kev brings out a few duffle bags for me to load in the car while Dad searches the back for the twenty-thou. But there's no cash. Kev told me later he had to urge Dad to hurry.

Standing over the victim, Dad extended his gun and asked, "Where's the money?"

The victim writhed for wiggle room. Facedown, he answered, "What money?"

"The sign outside says you buy gold. Where's the money you buy it with?" Dad asked.

"There's no cash," the man replied.

Kev told me later he touched Dad on the shoulder, grabbing without pulling. "Let's go," he mouthed.

Dad holstered his gun and followed Kev out the door. I already have the car pulled up. We drive off, passing a police cruiser on the way to the highway. We walked out with just over twenty grand in merchandise, a monumental failure compared to other jobs. Dad announces yet another deadline for these jobs, another goal he says we will meet and then quit while ahead, after Kev voices his concern about the risk outweighing the reward.

"Methuen will be better. Then we'll stop. Just one more decent-sized one and that'll be it." I know he's lying, that this announcement is just to pacify Kev. I begin to wonder if he ever intends to stop.

Dad's next idea is born of his excitement over the fiscal possibilities of insurance fraud, something he doesn't need Kev for, only me to discover a faux break-in over thanksgiving break. While he's away with Grandma basking in the warm Hawaiian sun, I'm to drive to his house and discover the break-in he set up before he left.

The Set-up

Dad invites me to lunch at the condo, which is code for an excuse to discuss the next robbery endeavor. He's in work clothes when I arrive: jeans and a plain solid-color T-shirt. When I was growing up, Dad only wore two types of clothes: suits and work clothes. There were no variations. Dad was always either working or working on something, and so he never slipped out of work attire or abandoned the persona other dads left behind after a long day, when they would come home, crack a beer and transmogrify into larger, hairier versions of their teenage selves. Mr. Burns across the street donned khakis and a shirt with something offbeat like "I sucked oysters at Gilly's" or "Have a nice f---ing day." Mr. Dowd wore Bermuda shorts and a Red Sox shirt that his wife claimed could walk around on its own.

As a teenager, I watched this duality with great interest. I took note of how, by Monday morning, the neighborhood dads were all back in their work garb, dragging the trash from the garage, bending in a way that avoided contact with their neatly pressed pants, their ties flung over their shoulders. By contrast, my dad approached the weekend as if he were switching jobs, one for another. I also noted at a tender age that he has only four modes: eat, sleep, sell, and build.

When I reach the condo, a tarp covers the front door. There is a wheel barrow half filled with cement. The contents of the other half fills crevices between slabs of granite in the walkway. The remnants of a cord of wood lay strewn around the stump they were split on. The rest of the wood is neatly stacked in the basement. Inside, the couch cushions lay on the floor with the covers pulled off. The freezer is open and defrosting.

The front door creaks, then snaps open. Shards of wood speckle the carpet as Dad stands draped under the tarp holding a crowbar.

"Boy, that was easier than I thought it was going to be. So what do you think?" he asks.

The house, usually so neatly kept, is in complete disarray. "Nancy gave me all the details of what her place looked like after she was broken into. All I have to do is pry the safe up from the floor upstairs and we're good to go," he continues. "After Thanksgiving dinner with your mom, you'll come here and discover the break-in." He pours a glass of water and gulps it down, sitting after drawing the shades. "Then I want you to go next door to Doug's and ask him to use his phone to call 911. It might be a good idea to tell them that you think you heard a noise, that you think the robbers are still in the house."

"Dad, do you think this might be a little too close to home?" I ask. "I mean, the place will be crawling with cops."

"I wouldn't worry about it, son. I've already taken everything out of the house, and what I didn't take someplace else is safely locked up downstairs. Relax. With this job, we'll easily clear twenty to thirty grand cash, all ours. Billy's not in on this one. This and Methuen and I think we're good. We'll stop."

The street is dead quiet, everyone away for the holiday, as I pull into the cul-de-sac and up the driveway. The sky is eerily clear on this unseasonably warm Thanksgiving Day. It rained earlier, so the streets have a sheen. I walk to the door, feign surprise, and run to Doug's across the street.

While he retrieves his cordless, I stare at the house, convinced that it stares back, hoping its poker face is more convincing than mine. A few minutes later, a police cruiser slithers up the street. I meet the officer at the foot of the driveway and reiterate what I told the 911 operator: "I came home and saw the door was smashed, and then I heard a noise inside."

He unholsters his sidearm and guides me back towards Doug's house. With flashlight in hand and gun at the ready, he then returns to Dad's and searches through the house. I want to confess just to alleviate what I assume is a cop's greatest fear: going toe-to-toe with an armed suspect.

When he emerges, other cops show up. Soon, the house swarms with cops. One dusts for prints and others just walk around, and I know that suspicions arise. "Someone was in here a long time," says the one with three stripes on his sleeve and thirty extra pounds, evidence he hasn't walked a beat in years. His only job seems to be manufacturing witticisms that are not all that witty. "Yep. Whoever was in here sure took their time." His sideways glances at me, at whatever it was that tipped him off to the fact that this was an inside job, make me wonder what nuances of breaking and entering were overlooked in Dad's planning.

No one else says a word. They all mill about as if communicating telepathically. In the end, the fat one tells me that we'll be hearing from a detective. They leave me alone with their dust covering surfaces they thought might reveal the identity of the perpetrator. It's a good thing they didn't dust me, I think.

I receive a phone call the next day. "This is Detective Connolly at the Nashua Police Department. I was wondering if you could come down here this morning and look at some photos. We think we know who broke into your home, and I'd like to see if you recognize him."

"Why would I recognize him? I wasn't there when the house was robbed, and my father was away." I say this adamantly, hoping to avoid the trip.

"Well, maybe you've seen him around. The kid we like for this is a known felon and lives close to your father," he replies, refusing to take no for an answer.

I show up at the station at ten and am ushered into the back where an elevator takes me to an office not much bigger than a walk-in closet. The walls are stark white. A single rotary phone sits on the wooden table flanked by two chairs.

Detective Connolly is built like a bulldog with a V-tapered back that looks all the more expansive because it is supported by beanpole legs. He breezes in and opens a manila file with the police report on the break-in and looks it over before asking, "Where's your brother?"

"I don't know." I answer, recalling what I saw in a movie once: *Name, rank, and serial number — that's the answer to every question they ask you.*

"Really?" he says. "I do."

"What's this have to do with my father's house getting robbed?" I ask.

"Because maybe he's in town and he's the one who broke in."

"My brother? I don't think so."

"No? Why not?"

"Because my brother would never do that to my father," I answer. "Besides, he has a key. Why would he break in?" I then remind myself to clam up.

"I'm just telling you what we know. He's in town and witnesses say they saw him at your father's on Thanksgiving Day."

"That's crazy. I know he's nowhere near here and couldn't possibly have broken into my father's house. It's impossible. I can prove it."

"I thought you didn't know where he was," Detective Connolly says.

"Obviously, I know where he is, and there's no way he did this."

"So he's far away?"

"He can't get much further away than he is right now," I reply.

"Got any way of proving that?" he asks as if he really wants to absolve my brother of the accusation.

"Sure. I'll call him up and you can hear for yourself." I take the offered receiver and dial Kev's Florida number. Of course, it being two hours prior to noon, there's no way Kev will answer. I hang up realizing the trap. They trace the call and now have a lock on him.

"Okay, so he's not around here. Then who could've broken into your Dad's house?" Detective Connolly asks while taking out a legal pad and jotting something illegible down.

"How should I know? I thought you had a suspect?" I squirm over the phone call, outraged that I fell for the trick.

"What about you? Maybe you did it," the detective says, pointing the capped end of his Bic pen at me.

"Me?" I ask. "That's ridiculous."

"You think so? The neighbors say they saw you at the house a few days ago, loading stuff into your car." The detective's eyes thin to a slit. He taps the pen on the legal pad as if it were set to the appropriate length of time for an innocent person to answer.

"Really? Like maybe they saw some suitcases and a carry on? I drove my father to the airport. That's what they saw."

The cop chicken scratches something else before asking, "Will you take a lie detector and say that you didn't rob the house?"

"Absolutely," I respond, but an inner dialogue starts. While the detective interrogates me, I interrogate myself. Did I rob the house? Technically no. But can I pass a lie detector?

"You'll take one now?" he asks again.

"Sure. I've got nothing to hide. I've been sober almost a year."

"Sober? You drank?"

"Drank, smoked, snorted — you name it," I say while he jots something else.

"Yeah? You bought drugs here in Nashua?"

"Only once. There's not a lot of drugs around here. At least I didn't know where to get them." More notes. At some point I lean back and slouch. "I got most of my drugs down in Mass."

"From who?" he asks.

It dawns on me that he got me to squawk. I tell him I think I should have a lawyer present. To which Detective Connolly replies, "Yeah, maybe you should."

By the time he lets me go, I am wracked with guilt and need to talk to Dad. I call the hotel he's staying at and insist he call back using the payphone number I give him.

"What is it, son?" Dad asks. The sounds of waves crash in the background.

"This cop is fucking relentless. He accused me of robbing the house and I'm sure he'll want to talk to you." I hold my hand over the payphone receiver, worried I'm being watched or that I will be overheard.

"So let him talk. He doesn't have shit on us. I wouldn't worry. That's what they do. You didn't tell them anything they could use, did you?" he asks.

"No, nothing." I leave out the part about Kev and the phone call.

"Then, when I get back to town, I'll talk to him. No biggie. Relax, son. It'll be fine," he says before we segue into small talk about his trip. Hawaii is beautiful but expensive, he says, and my grandmother is having a great time. He says he'll be home in a few days.

Our conversation fails to soothe me. I can feel Detective Connolly's piercing eyes on me everywhere.

When Dad comes home and meets with the detective, he doesn't report anything close to what I went through. The meeting is cordial, a formality, Detective Connolly tells him. He makes no mention of my brother or me, and he even presents photos of possible suspects.

Dad gets to work filling his phony insurance claim for items that were taken during the robbery. Billy gets receipts for a gold Rolex, a five carat diamond, a two carat sapphire, and ten thousand in bearer bonds, all of which are covered by Dad's homeowners insurance and are replaced within days of filing his claim. With the ink still drying on the police report, Dad moves on to the next job as if he's following a how-to on armed robbery: Step two---Keep going.

It isn't the location, a store on the quiet end of a strip mall, that is appealing. It isn't the set up. We have no intention of taking a thing from the store. Dad proposes that by robbing the salesman only, it will look like the owner is in on it, that way when the cops investigate the crime they'll suspect the owner and never even look for us.

It's the ease that appeals to us. No adrenaline. No unmitigated sense of dread. Kev and I laugh over slices of pizza bought next door while Dad makes business calls from his cell. At ten, a man exits his vehicle with a small travel dolly full of cases and enters the store. I drive up. Dad and Kev go in. I watch the incoming traffic, keeping an eye on the store. Dad holds up the salesman while Kev keeps his gun on the owner. A few minutes later, we're speeding away. We wipe down the rental and drive off in Dad's Maxima. Relaxed. Joking. Oblivious.

When we reach the rotary that will take us back to the highway, we pass a police cruiser responding to the call. The passenger side cop gives us a look, but I blow it off. After five years of pulling these jobs, I am numb to potential dangers, or maybe I'm burnt out. At this point, I am unsure of the difference.

Both Dad and I go to work afterward. I leave Kev with his bag of weed and a delivery on the way. Minus the wait time, it takes us four minutes for close to twenty grand in merchandise. No one mentions it is piffle next to Burlington. Not even Dad.

The Jig Is Up

Another spring break and a much needed respite from school. It's tough juggling the internship with school and third shift on the weekends. I sit down in the recliner with a steaming cup of coffee and several double chocolate chunk cookies.

News Center Five's top story is about the arrest of a local man in connection with jewelry store robberies netting close to three million. The phone rings. I stare at the screen. Detective Connolly leads a man draped in a windbreaker into the Nashua Police Station. Even with his face concealed, there's no doubt the cuffed man is Dad. I recognize the gait, the long strides, grace under pressure, but most notably, the lack of panic. What Dad lacks in that regard I more than make up for. I stand, then sit, and stand again, suddenly aware that the windows are open. The phone rings incessantly it seems, without pause. I close the windows, shut the shades, and switch to another station. All three networks run the arrest as a top story. Shots of the front of Dad's house and a table full of jewelry I know to be costume flash on the screen. Detective Connolly fills the television with a mocking expression meant solely for me. He uses cop pronouns: the suspect this is allegedly that and Connolly won't comment on whether more arrests are expected. But his smirk lets me know he's coming for me.

The phone stops, or at least returns to intervals. I answer just to get it to shut up, relieved it isn't my mother or grandmother but Nancy. "Your Dad's been arrested," she says.

"It's on the fucking five o'clock news, for Christ's sake." I begin losing it.

"He was on his way to pick up Chinese food when they pulled him over. He was on his way here afterwards. He just called me." I can tell she's shaken, and so I calm down.

"What did they arrest him for?" I ask.

"They haven't given him specific charges, but you can guess what the charges will be from the news."

I say, "It's probably not a good idea to talk on the phone. I'm heading to the house. I'll call you later," and I hang up without saying goodbye.

I slither into my car as if doing so unseen and drive conspicuously slowly. The usually short forty minute ride takes me an hour and fifteen minutes. When I pull up to the house, there is a cruiser parked outside. I ignore it and pull into the driveway.

The officer intercepts me in the walkway and asks where I am going. "Into my house, officer. Is there a problem?"

"You live here?" he asks.

"Yes."

"You got ID that proves that?"

"I have identification, but it has my mother's address on it."
I offer it to him. He looks it over, turning it towards the waning
light.

"Sorry, but I can't let you in unless you have this address
on your license. Besides, detectives will be here in a few minutes
to search the house. You better get on out of here," he warns.

I see on the news that they found all the costume jewelry in
the house that we planned on throwing away. But the safe
downstairs has more than enough evidence to sink us. I ponder
driving a few streets away and sneaking in through the backdoor,
but instead, I drive back home. Mom is working late. Dad calls
collect from Valley Street Jail in Manchester.

"Hi, son."

"Jesus Christ, Dad. What are we going to do?"

"Calm down, son. First off, I need a lawyer. Is there any
way you can find me one? I have another court date next week and
need legal counsel to find out exactly what they have so I know
what we're dealing with here." He's cool, calm, and collected. I
can barely hear him above all the background noise of the jail, a
noise that casts fear into every fiber of my being.

"Dad, are you okay?" I fight back tears.

"Oh, I'm fine, son. Not exactly the best of accommodations
here, but I'm fine." His nonchalance runs so counter to the
magnitude of the day's events that it seems surreal.

"Can I send you anything?" I ask, now on the verge of
weeping uncontrollably.

"There's a commissary here. You can imagine the food's not very good, but if you could send a few dollars, that'd help."

"I will. And I'll send a lawyer as soon as I can, Dad."

"Thanks, son. I'll talk to you soon."

He makes no mention of Kev. There is no coded warning that he should be notified and take precautions. No mention of Grandma and how to handle her or what to tell anyone else asking why his face is all over the television news and on the front page of every paper. Just get me a lawyer, and send me commissary money, he asked. I do both.

There is a laundry list of attributes that describe my mother, not all of them positive, but stupid isn't one of them. In the initial twenty-four hours after Dad's arrest, I adopt shrugged shoulders and claim to be clueless as to why he has been arrested. My act pulls the wool over Grandma's eyes, but Mom is more savvy, and bullshitting her is no small feat.

There is something sickeningly satisfying in her step as she helps me clean out Dad's house just before the bank forecloses. Bills stack so high the post office stops delivering once the mail reaches the brim of the box. Mom's giddiness stems from a jealousy I'm familiar with, so apparent growing up it was hard not to share her jubilation. Dad went off to live the high life after the divorce. To his credit, he never missed an alimony or child support payment, but Dad's success always made Mom resentful.

Unfortunately, any sick satisfaction derived from Dad's downfall paled in comparison to the nosedive her heart took once Detective Connolly arrested Kev, personally making the trip to Florida to haul him back.

It was after a long day of moving when he called from the Middlesex County Jail. He was charged with armed robbery. It had been more than a decade since her eyes were a constant state of bloodshot. But now she cries on a dime, taking pity on me but avoiding the topic at the same time. At lunch, in a quiet neighborhood greasy spoon, she asks, "Are you mixed up in this?"

The impulse to lie is ingrained, but I fail miserably. I wish for rails to hold as I nod, affirming her worst fear. My words deliver a wrecking ball blow to her chest as she collapses, slumping as if I kicked her in the ribs. "How did this happen? Is it because I kicked you out?" She is referring to when I was 18 and she was newly sober, unable to keep me in line. I was on a cruise control by then, held captive by my anger, my hurt buried beneath mounds of coke, weed, and pills. It was her first of many attempts to get me into rehab.

"Mom, you can't blame this on yourself. We did this on our own."

"HE did this on HIS own, you mean." Not since I was a kid have I seen anger this raw in my mother. Her left eye twitches and I know she'll kill him if she gets close enough.

"They'll come for me at some point, I'm sure." I add.

"We'll deal with it when it happens. Oh God, what are we going to do?"

"I'm sorry, Mom."

"Me too."

To help avoid the gnawing paranoia I feel with every step, I take the unwanted holiday shifts so that I can pay for the basement apartment I rent from a friend at work. Staying at Mom's was too risky. I snuck into Dad's house days prior to evacuating Mom's, surprised to find that, after three separate searches, the cops never found the safe downstairs. The combination was hidden inside a wall switch in Dad's room, folded methodically and placed next to a bunch of wires. I relieved the safe of its contents, which included cash, loose diamonds, and a few rolls of incidentals we kept from each robbery.

The next day, my phone rings, waking me. Only three people have the number: work, Mom, and Dawn, my ex-girlfriend.

"Don't ever have jewelry sent to this address!" Dawn barks loudly. I have to hold the receiver away from my ear.

"What? I didn't. What are you talking about?"

"A UPS driver just showed up here with a package for you. Who sent it, Billy? I can't believe you had it mailed here." She then rambles for a bit and I can't even get a word in.

"Are you done? I didn't send anything to your apartment. What's in the package?" I ask, wondering if it was indeed Billy who sent the package.

Because Detective Connolly arrested Nancy outside the place she worked a week ago, I shaved my head and, except to drive to work or the gym, refused to go out. The stress is stifling. So as Dawn tells me about the package, my sense of self preservation kicks in and I know deep down its Detective Connolly getting crafty.

"Where is the package now?" I ask once she calms down.

"I told the guy I'd take it and give it to you when I saw you, but he said it required an ID," she says, transitioning from accusatory to suspicious mid-sentence.

I tell her, "It's probably a trick the cops are playing, Dawn, and now you've led them here. Nice job," I say, and I hang up.

I am slightly freaked for just a moment and then decide to go about my day, knowing that, if they have a lock on me, there's nothing I can do to escape. I plan to head to the gym to workout and then run errands. By the time I reach the gym, the sky is overcast with thick gray clouds. The blistering cold stifles any wind. I trudge through a workout and head home to lay low.

The lane drop before the Merrimac Bridge frequently causes heavy congestion, and the left lane slows to a stop while the right lane merges. This day, the constant rise and fall of brake lights lulls me into a trance.

The car in front of me lurches forward. A streak of maroon darts into my periphery before it registers as a sedan. It cuts off the right lane and nearly clips my bumper before filling the space between me and the car in front. I recognize his face before I recognize the loaded weapon pointed at me.

"GET YOUR HANDS WHERE I CAN SEE THEM! NOW!" Detective Connolly shouts.

Eternity passes while I take in the scene. The players stand out, the final act choreographed with such precision it dismantles any illusion I was ever a step ahead of them. Two marked police cruisers close off the bridge in the opposite direction. Officers stand outside their cars with pistols aimed carefully, and helicopter blades slice the air somewhere above. Detective Connolly repeats demands for me to exit the vehicle and lay face down on the ground. I sit for a few seconds longer, deciding whether to throw myself over the bridge's high railings, confident I'll be shot before clearing the top and so won't need to worry about any pain upon landing.

I step out of the car, and a flurry of activity ensues around me. Detective Connolly pins me to the hood of the car, plucks me from the free world and everything else I gave up the moment I decided to help Dad.

It is midnight when Detective Connolly finally comes to get me from the holding cell. "Let's go," he says, motioning for me to take the lead out of the cell. Then he directs me to an elevator.

Back in his interrogation room, the same manila folder sits on the same table I sat at when I was here before, but I note that the folder is much thicker this time.

"We arrested Billy earlier. The grand jury indicted you two at the same time. Billy already talked. He's pointing fingers like crazy at you and your family. I'm all wrapped up here with your dad and brother, so I'm not going to charge you for being an accomplice to that bogus break-in at your Dad's house." He stops abruptly and sits back. "But if you had something to say, I'd consider telling the Attorney General down in Mass that you were cooperative. It might bode well for you at trial."

I know that Detective Connolly has all he needs without my testimony, and I simply offer my name, rank, and serial number. The next morning, a bear claw and a cold cup of black coffee sit on the floor outside my cell. Everyone arrested the night before is lined up at the intake desk. I'm the only one shackled. We're loaded into a paddy wagon and driven to District Court.

Mom is in the courtroom with black circles under her eyes. I sign papers, waiving my right to fight extradition to Massachusetts. The clerk explains that Mass has seven days to claim me. They then ship me to the Valley Street Jail that afternoon, the same place they're holding Dad.

My street clothes are exchanged for an orange jumpsuit and underwear two sizes too big and an officer escorts me to unit 4-2. The guard pulls me aside. "Your dad is in the block across the hall. As a rule, you're not allowed near the windows, so I'm giving you a warning now. If you see him, ignore the urge to signal him or wave in any way. If you're caught, you'll go to segregation." He ends with, "Your dad's fine. He said to tell you hello."

I don't have time to feel the sting of insincerity in Dad's brief message. "Hello" does nothing to help me figure out how to make it through my first night behind bars. Despite the guard's warning, I can't stop focusing on the block across the hall. Any movement garners my attention, and a few minutes before lockdown, I catch a glimpse of him walking across the unit. He's either oblivious or heeding the warning not to establish contact with me.

Time passes tortuously slow. An attempted suicide breaks the monotony — an inmate is caught hanging himself from a bed sheet. I hear the man cry, "Please! I no want to be here," in a thick Hispanic accent.

After morning count, the doors open and I follow the crowd to a window where trays of runny eggs are shoved at us while word passes through the grapevine that the attempted suicide was in for molesting his nine year-old stepdaughter.

I give my breakfast away and return to my cell. After morning count, the doors open, and I take a seat at one of the metal tables, keeping an eye on the block next door. Two inmates nearby have a newspaper spread out on in front of them. Both chuckle when I catch their eye. "This you?" asks one of them.

I walk over and see the article on page two: "Second Son Arrested in Jewelry Heist Ring." The paper is local to New

Hampshire, and I cringe at the thought that everyone at work will see it. I scan the details. They spelled my name wrong, report I am a former crack addict, and mention Dad and Kev. The two inmates shake their heads. "Damn, man. That's heavy. You'll get seven years for this, easy." I'm too distracted by the image of Dad filling the window across the hall to respond.

I notice that he's lost a few pounds. His jumpsuit is neater than mine, brighter. I squint to see him clearly, but the guard catches on and shoots an unmistakable look of warning. I stand my ground, caring little for the threat of the Segregation Unit. They can tar and feather me for all I care. Nothing is tearing me away from the window, but Dad sees the guard and quickly wanders off.

It's the mundane that hurts the most, the everyday activities taken for granted at home but that take on some kind of perverse energy now. Showering, watching TV, and using the phone are all unbearable. I adopt a morbid curiosity about the attempted suicide as I sit on the second floor tier. I try to figure out how he hung himself with nothing in the ceiling to tie off on. Did he use the bunk? There's no other way, I conclude.

I lack strength for such exercises in the how-to's and the what-if's, let alone for this strange world of bars and cinderblock walls. Dad has the brains. Kev has the brawn. I am ill-equipped for this life. I realize that jail is not a world I can weather. I make one last call to Mom, a conscious goodbye, an unconscious plea for help.

The operator connects us. My mother's voice dispels any notion of ending my life, if only to spare heaping more grief upon her.

"Mom?" I ask so as not to unload on a wrong number.

"What is it, sweetheart?"

"I don't think I can do this."

"Do what, hon?"

"Time."

"I know. Believe me, I'm in there with you. We'll make it through this, somehow."

Hope seems an utterly unacceptable option, but hearing her distress, I compromise. "Listen, Mom. I'll make a deal with you. If you hold on, then so will I."

"Deal," she answers without a pause.

"That means, if you slip, even a little, know that you'll be taking me with you."

"And vice versa?"

"Yup."

"Deal. Count me in."

"Ok. I gotta go, Mom. They're locking us in."

"Alright. I'll be out to see you soon. And son?"

"Yeah, Mom."

"You saved my life tonight."

"You saved mine too, Mom."

Two giant bags of meat in uniform transport me to Massachusetts. At arraignment, my court-appointed lawyer's jaw plummets when the judge sets bail at five million. I'm whisked to the jail on the seventeenth floor where a conversation with a shoeless seventeen-year-old distresses me to say the least. He uses the word "accidentally" to describe how he killed his pregnant girlfriend by kicking her in the stomach as if it's a common abortion option.

"They took my shoes, I guess, cuz I stomped her to death," he says.

I take note he still had his feet. Taking his shoes is tantamount to taking a sheath but leaving the sword.

My ears perk when Kev's voice reaches me in the holding cell. Through his connections, he arranges for us to work together in the kitchen until my grandmother posts my bail. The lawyer she hires gets my bail reduced, partly because professors at school and coworkers at the hospital write letters to the judge.

When I get out on bail, the decision to relapse is easy. There's no reason to stay clean. Mark fires me, citing hospital policy: no employee with outstanding felony charges is allowed to work with patients. With no other support system than work, or at least none that I choose to utilize, I end up right back where I left off: on the receiving end of a crack pipe.

After three weeks of draining my savings, I stop again, without meetings and without rehab. I just stop. I dive back into the new semester as if nothing happened, manage to get another job at a rehab in Dover, New Hampshire, and spend the summer working and acting as if doom isn't looming above my head like a million ton bag of shit, like the storm of the century about to let loose only on me. No one notices the black cloud that pours continuously over me, the threatening thunder that drowns out any long-term plans.

Two days before what I think is another formality in a long line of court dates, my lawyer calls and says, "I think it's time to discuss our options. I think we should take what the judge offers tomorrow. A guilty verdict at trial might get you double digits."

Before the hearing, he hands me the Attorney General's sentencing report that recommends four and a half years in the Massachusetts Department of Corrections. I nearly pass out.

The words resurrect a fear planted during my stay in County Jail where the word "upstate" conjured visions of gang rape in showers and the searing kiss of a rusty metal shank. County lockup is where I learned the distinction between jail and prison, between purgatory and hell.

My lawyer negotiates the number down to three years. Pleading guilty is a long, drawn out process of answering questions about my state of mind. Am I competent to plead guilty? Am I under the influence of drugs or alcohol? Kev is forced to answer the same questions, and then we're shackled and led to a waiting transport van. Kev is behind me. His sentencing report recommended he do fifteen but the judge agreed to eight. Twenty or thirty links of stainless steel between our feet hinder our pace, limiting our gait to a shuffle. The transport officer opens the back doors of the van that will take us to the Massachusetts Correctional Institution in Concord, MCI Concord.

"Step up!" the guard barks. His girth is just as intimidating as his obvious contempt for us.

The height of the step seems infinite compared to the amount of slack allowed by the shackles. "You're joking, right?" I ask.

He grabs my shoulder and "assists" me into the van. His help lands me on my stomach on the floor, where I flop like a trout in the bottom of a boat. The officer doesn't assist Kev, I assume because they share the same propensity for converting calories into brute strength.

The doors seal us inside. I can see the free world through the grate of the steel cage. We joke about Kev's refusal to address the judge with actual words rather than grunts.

"Are you under the influence of any drugs or alcohol that would impede your understanding of the guilty plea you are entering today?" the judge asked.

"Mmm," my brother answered, as if he was multitasking: answering the question and clearing his dry throat at the same time.

The judge got agitated. "You will address the court using the vernacular — yes or no!"

"Vernacular" threw Kev off his mental drift as his lawyer scrambled to reiterate what the judge meant. "Just say 'yes' or 'no,'" he spouted, his fee for translating condescension into caveman a paltry two hundred per hour.

As we approach our new home, I catch a glimpse of the sixty foot wall that surrounds the prison through my grated perspective. A guard tower sits atop the corner, and swirls of razor-wire, designed specifically to tighten at the slightest sign of tension, glisten along the top of the wall.

The van stops, doors slam, and thick-soled boots pound the pavement. The doors fly open, and the dank space inside the van floods with sunshine. "Let's go, ladies!" our chauffeur barks.

We're led through the visitors' waiting room and pass through two large steel doors. The hallway is a length of steel, concrete, and thick ceramic tile, all buffed to a sheen.

Another uniformed officer ushers us into a room. "Strip down and place all your garments into the bags."

"Jeez. They sure don't waste any time. They just violate me right off the bat and get it over with," I say, only half joking.

"Face front," the guard snaps as if he's training a savage animal that is browbeaten and forced to oblige. "Palms up, open your mouth, lift your tongue!" He shines a flashlight into our mouths. "Run your fingers through your hair. Turn. Lift your feet. Bend and spread."

He tells us to get dressed. The collared shirt, pants, and coat we are provided all have a sandpapery feel. The door at the end of the hallway is then opened, the belly of the beast exposed. From within, the outer wall casts a shadow no matter how high the noontime sun ascends. The absence of vibrant colors gives everything a surreal black and white feeling. Color is absorbed by the predominance of brick and mortar, swallowed up, denatured, and regurgitated.

We're ushered to another building, placed in a circular cell, and handed bag lunches, the Department of Correction's version of sustenance. Inside the foil wrap are sandwiches. The meat, possibly baloney, is a quarter inch thick. The bread's texture suggests toasting but lacks the golden brown hue of electric crisping. No, this crunch is from petrified grains that are just short of fuzzy penicillin.

My name is called while Kev polishes off the last of my sandwich. My stomach churns. Nerves and two bites of rancid meat battle in my digestive tract. I approach the cop at the intake desk. He snaps an impromptu photo of me, laminates it, and refers to me by my con number.

"W55906, step up to the printer." I expect a Hewlett Packard but get the latest fingerprinting technology. "Roll 'em across the screen," he commands. I acquiesce. "Any scars, marks, or tattoos?"

"No."

"Go to the J building, you're in J-1," are his final words to me. I cradle my bedding and pass through the buzzing security doors into a courtyard.

Intimidations, slurs, a new kind of insult for my tender ears drop from the slits that pose as windows. Their echo finds no escape from walls so adept at confining that even sound can't find a way out of them. "Yo-yo, a new fish," someone shouts from a window on the top floor.

"New fish? He look green. That ain't no new fish — that's fresh meat," shouts someone from another window on the second floor.

"He look sweet. Com 'ere new fish. I ain't gonna bite cha"

"Yo, he say he ain't gonna bite 'im."

"I'm gonna enjoy gettin' me suma that."

My pace quickens. The volley continues as I fall for the oldest trick in the book.

"Hey, yo. You dropped somethin'."

I turn to find only my failed sensibilities and the rancorous laughter of thugs with nothing better to do.

Through the window in the door to J-1, I see a lone CO sitting behind a desk. I pause briefly to take it all in. The unit is three tiers high, each tier a row of numbered cells. The door buzzes after my presence captures the attention of the CO.

"I'm Rock, but don't use the name to address me. I won't respond. This is an orientation block, which means, until you see the classification board, you're locked up twenty-three hours a day."

Rock's enormity makes me wonder if he was manufactured from the same raw material that erected the building. His tattoos are more like livestock brands, bright red lightning bolts that taper from his elbows, a warning that he is not to be trifled with.

"You're in cell two. Your bed is to be made at all times. You'll clean the cell once a day. If a fight breaks out and you can't make it to your cell, just drop to the floor and wait until the move team comes. You'll probably get lugged. If they settle it and you're cleared, they'll send you back. If not…" He shrugs, an empty gesture made all the more empty because he lacks the neck required to complete the act.

I make my way to my cell. They're numbered right to left. Cell two is in the lower right corner. Rock hits the switch and the door electrically hums open.

The cell is no bigger than a walk-in closet. My cellmate is Hispanic with short curly hair. He sits on the bottom bunk chewing his nails, biting off pieces and spitting them indiscriminately into the air. He looks all bark and no bite. By process of elimination, I toss my bedding on the top. Through the tiny vertical window, I see my brother walk through the courtyard.

The bunks are welded metal slabs bolted to off-white walls, the floor an indiscriminate gray. A desk, more like a metal shelf, conceals a stainless steel stool that swivels on an iron hinge. The toilet/sink combo is a tribute to efficiency, sculpted by minimalists. The cell's isolation contributes to the uncanny feeling that the prison is submerged, plunged deep into the world's unconscious, like a bad memory, selectively forgotten.

I spread out the sheets and take extra care not to disturb my disgruntled cellmate. When I'm finished, I lay on top, only a few feet from the ceiling. The mattress feels like a burlap sack filled with rubble. All the bedding bears the Department of Correction's stamp of approval — "Fire Retardant."

The logical part of me chews on my sentence in an attempt to break it down for assimilation, like a mouthful of food. Three years. Thirty six months. One thousand ninety five days. My throat constricts and my gag reflex warns that any attempt to swallow will be overridden. My brain's only option is to log off, regroup, and sort it out in slumber.

Projected into sleep while in full sensory overload, I dream of being home. The smell of early morning, fresh-cut grass, and the occasional exhaust fumes of a hurried commuter waft through the window. I walk outside and inhale, arms outstretched. The world around me opens, prepared to return the embrace. Suddenly the screen goes blank as I'm roused by the clank of electric doors grinding open. I get up slowly. The transition back to reality is excruciating.

Rock stands by the door and hands out passes, tagging each inmate as if we were packages rolling down a conveyer belt. Outside, I keep pace with the current so as not to get swept up or steamrolled. I search the river of blue denim for Kev, who has been locked up for over a year and has more experience traversing these waters. I need advice, direction.

The blue is channeled back into single file as the line forms for chow. Cops pepper the crowd like buoys. Most are dressed in regular blue uniforms, others in all black. In typical assembly line fashion, I am handed a tray by a fellow inmate and another shoves a bowl of soup at me. At the end of the line, a CO hands me a spoon from a suitcase.

On my tray are a bowl of vegetable soup, the veggies wilted, nearly liquefied; a flaky, completely unappetizing, white mass I assume is fish; and a massive square of frosted cake. I find Kev sitting with a group of guys he did county time with. Kev's diabetic meal has a piece of fresh fruit on it, a stark contrast to the dreary soup and sewer fish. One of Kev's companions, Joey, fishes a dead cockroach out of his soup.

"EEEWWW, fucking disgusting!" He holds the pickled insect between his bony thumb and forefinger. Joey's brain runs like an over-wound clock, ten minutes ahead and gaining. "Fuck this! I'm gonna complain!" His clothes hang like drapery over a breezy window and give his movements a ghostlike succinctness.

As his lips move, his hands accentuate an impassioned plea, and yet he fails to capture the CO's attention. The cop looks down at the dead bug Joey so poignantly places on the end of his spoon.

"Get that thing away from me," the guard commands. Another cop, one dressed in black, flanks Joey.

"Why is he in a different uniform?" I ask Kev.

"He's an IP, Inner Perimeter Security — don't fuck with 'em."

"Thanks for the tip," I reply. I had no intention of doing so.

The cop addressing Joey says, "Look, for all I know you put the damn thing in there yourself. Keep pissing me off and I'll lug you," loud enough for everyone to hear.

"Stupid prick," Joey mutters when he is back at the table.

"Wrap it up. The food's not getting any tastier!" the IP yells to the crowd. The command rouses everyone.

I get up and push my tray into the lengthwise window near the door. Joey jumps into the sea of trays to retrieve my spoon. "You're not getting very far without that spoon, bro." He hands it to me and drops his into the guarded metal box next to the door.

I notice the buildings while I walk back to the J's. The only one not surrounded by its own razor wire fence is the chapel. Purposefully sunk into the ground, the house of worship seems shamed, burrowing to hide from the hypocrisy of its very presence here in hell.

Back on the block, Rock bellows, "Five minutes to count!"

Slippery Pete

J-1 has a row of phones fixed to the wall near the stairs. Three are in use. Inmates, huddled close to the cradle, press the receiver to their ears. I pick up the only free phone and dial my grandmother. All I hear is the hollow sound of distant oceans.

"You need a pin number," my cellmate informs me as I pass him. "You need to fill out a request and get your numbers approved. What'd you think you could just pick up the phone and call whoever?"

"How do I get a pin number?"

"Get a form." he says before zipping off into our cell. I look around the area Rock occupies for a cubby hole or mail slot where forms might be kept. But before I can find one Rock activates the door controls, indicating it's time for lockdown.

During my first week, he lugs three people who fail to make it to their cells in time. The inmates segregate according to race with the occasional group of varietals considered untouchable, those pegged as sex offenders or rats. Going near them tells the rest of the population that you side with them.

I know one of the block's runners and part of the prison's permanent work force as Pete, a sex offender and therefore, untouchable. Concord's designation as a classification prison makes it every convict's first stop. By law an inmate is entitled to see the class board every three months to determine his security risk. Most don't want a permanent work assignment at Concord because other prisons offer better privileges.

Every DOC has a canteen. With money sent from the outside, inmates can purchase the comforts of home like toiletries, candy, and snacks. Workers have the luxury of purchasing a hotpot, allowing them to cook pasta and heat water for instant coffee.

Pete is Rock's gofer, running around all day, sweeping, mopping, dusting, and occasionally bringing hot water to those of us fortunate enough to order coffee. "*Runner!*" shouted from any given cell summons Pete, and depending on his mood, he delivers a piping hot plastic container of boiled water. Unfortunately the water is usually tainted, giving the coffee a funky, plastic aftertaste.

The epitome of debauchery, barren gums fail to dam Pete's tongue, and he slurs each syllable. His jailhouse tattoos resemble ink blots. A faded swastika on his right shoulder blade was apparently haphazardly imbedded with a sewing needle and pen ink.

Pete tells me he killed a man with a shotgun, shooting him point blank, and he claimed it was self-defense. A raised brow telegraphs my doubts, and he admits to leaving the barroom and returning with the gun. "Doesn't that prove premeditation?" I ask, my Cracker Jack law degree still reeking of caramel corn. I keep our conversation short, knowing that sympathizing with sex offenders makes me a target.

Given Pete's temperament, the eruption the next day doesn't surprise me. Just after lockdown, Pete and Rock exchange words. We all scramble to the door. Our vantage point makes it difficult to see, but Pete is pacing into his cell and out. Rock is at attention, immovable.

Pete's angry words bounce off the concrete and reach our door garbled. We fill in blanks where we can — something about a mop. Rock offers two options: calm down or face the move team. Pete calls his bluff. "Go ahead, you fucking military reject!"

Rock turns his back and Pete disappears from sight. "Rock's calling in the move team. This is going to be good," someone says.

Comments, like smoke, hard not to inhale, fill the block and float through the vents. *Yo, Pete done flipped his lid. Give 'em hell Pete. Rock don't take no shit, man. The move team gonna bundle him up.*

Chaos ensues. The percussive rhythm of rolling thunder fills the block like a stampede. Anxious fists pound on doors and drum up tension as Pete emerges from his cell with a bottle of baby oil.

The anarchists fall silent to the echo of boots marching with clocked precision. The move team reaches the block in two single file lines. Clad in executioner's black, each officer is synchronized with the collective. The plastic faceguards of their helmets gleam under the florescent light, flesh and bone secure under layers of protective material.

I concentrate on Pete. He steps sinisterly backward and sprays baby oil. Once the move team is inside, a hush blankets the block. Pete stands ready to face the consequences.

Rock manually unlocks the door with his key and holds it open. The move team's tight formation is led by clear shields that deliver a jolt of electricity that incapacitates on contact.

"He's in deep shit, man," my cellmate whispers.

The first two hit the baby oil slick and careen into the wall. Top heavy, they topple onto their shields. The middle two, now in front, stand on the precipice of the slick and feebly attempt to help their flailing counterparts. The team tightens their formation and takes shorter steps.

Take him! Get his legs! We hear the commotion through the vents. *Do not move! You're only making this worse!* Pete's coffee cup hits the floor, gets kicked out of the way, and tumbles onto the block. *Watch his other arm! Get it down! Cuffs! Cuffs! Get 'em tight!* They drag Pete out cuffed and slide him along the floor through the oil.

Back in formation, they lift Pete off the ground by his limbs. I can see the swastika veiled under his soaked cotton shirt, his muscles tense from the pressure.

My cellmate flops on his bunk — back to business as usual. Rock cracks open the cell of another runner and orders him to clean up the oil and pack Pete's things.

"Where do they take him?" I ask.

"The hole."

"The hole?"

"Yeah, the hole. You know, segregation? Tiny cell all to yourself. Locked down twenty-four, seven. No books, no movement, no nothing. Pete fucked himself too. The cops'll probably beat him down for that little stunt."

Migraines Out of Molehills

Rock's last words to me are, "Pack it up. Go to east down." The building he means is one I pass everyday on the way to chow. The building's rich history of housing a century's worth of inmates gives it a skeletal feel. The white stucco is distinct among the newer, post-inception, brick structures surrounding it. The three-by-three foot windows are panes of Plexiglas sectioned by thick wrought iron. The middle pane opens only a crack, enough for a person trapped inside to suffocate slowly during a fire. The outside screen is heavy steel mesh.

The heavy iron door has very little give and it takes all my weight to get the rusty hinges to budge. The door groans like a rickety old man forced to move beyond his range of motion, the creaks ricocheting throughout the building.

"What took you so long?" the sergeant asks, standing in the doorway of the hub.

I shrug. "You're in cell 243," he says on the tail end of clearing his throat.

Cell 243 is the second to last on the left. As the door grinds open, a diamond shaped swatch of sunlight spills into the hallway.

Inside, my new cellmate is lying on his bunk. Mat is clean cut, tall, and handsome, leaving the impression that his crime was non-violent. He doesn't seem to have it in him. Then I realize his assessment of me might be exactly the same.

The cells are much smaller than in the J's. Just outside our window, through two sets of chain link fence, is the yard. The sun overloads my sight and washes out the colors. My mind fills in the blanks: light blue shirts, dark blue denim pants, white T's, green grass, silver fences, stainless steel razor wire, and of course, the ever present gray concrete wall.

They always hang out together. The fat one is loud, jovial in the sense that he might not smash your face in. The other is quiet, capable, but only if provoked. I watch them from the periphery of the weight pit in the yard. The quiet one sees me; the fat one is oblivious. The quiet one gestures toward the weights strewn around them and allows me to work in. I do so, but I keep my distance, paranoid they'll think I "owe" them.

I take their generosity with a grain of salt. The risk outweighs the reward in working out here, but I need to engage in something familiar. The quiet one and the fat one talk, staying within earshot of each other. I'm jittery, careful not to reach for something at the same time as someone else. It feels good to tax my body with a workout.

The next day, I wait for the cell door to open so I can make it to the yard before anyone else, but the smaller inmates speed-walk past me. Frustrated, I burst into a run. Ahead, a guard blocks the entryway, screams at me, and sends me back to the block. I pass the guys who allowed me to work out in their midst the night before. The fat one laughs.

Back on the block, my cellmate packs his things. He is off to another prison. He leaves me some of his canteen and a coffee cup. The sergeant doesn't lock my door, and so I seize the opportunity to shower without unwanted company. I smell like a wet dog since my clothes came back from laundry feeling microwaved, burning hot outside and moist in the middle.

The fat one sees me hanging my clothes to dry, braces himself on the threshold and leans in. "Who runs in prison? Could you feel the tower guards' sights on you?" His rotund belly pokes under his shirt.

"I was just trying to get to the weights before everyone else."

"What, no cellie?"

"No. He shipped out this morning."

"Don't hurt yourself," he says, and he pushes off and slips into his cell as the doors close.

Before dinner, I get a new cellmate, Mike. His shirt is half tucked in and his shoes and socks are caked with mud. Hair sprouts from every available follicle. His stubble has stubble. He stands with limp wrists and talks with an exaggerated lisp. He slips off his shoes, climbs onto the bunk, and falls asleep. I'm sickened by the rank odor of his bare feet. He snores loud enough to miss the call for count.

I sit while the block sleeps, wrapped in a coarse blanket as fall takes the nightshift for a retiring summer. Sleep evades me, but even when it comes, I fight it. I wish Kev was in the bunk above, snoring. It is somehow soothing to know he's close by.

Movement across my face wakes me close to dawn. I jump and flick on the light. Cockroaches scurry while my cellmate blinks awake. I indiscriminately swat the floor with a shoe, chasing them under the bed. Mike clutches sheets to his chest, terrified. The jingle of keys grows louder. Flashlight shines in my eyes.

"What's the problem in there?"

"Nothing," I reply.

"It looks like there's a problem in there."

"No problem, right Mike?" He doesn't answer.

"Lights out. No more noise," the guard says, and he marches back to a nap or the crossword that entertained him prior.

I turn off the light and climb back in bed, still clutching my shoe. A slight tremble travels through the flimsy bed frame. Back and forth the frame starts to squeak. I fear an earthquake, until I realize Mike is masturbating.

I clear my throat. He stops, waits, and starts again. "You're fucking kidding me, right?" I blurt. I hear him flop into the fetal position. I feel badly that I snapped at him. I sit up and gaze out the window. There is no darkness anywhere, night frightened away by the preponderance of artificial light.

The next day, the fat one points me out to the quiet one, who agrees to let me work in again.

"As long as you don't run away with the weights," the fat one remarks. I learn that Smitty is in for parole violations because he just can't stay away from the booze. Mac is the quiet one, and he always speaks just loud enough. I peg him for Latino: dark features, pock-marked face, dark eyes, like he has fully dilated pupils that take in the world from a different perspective, perhaps seeing the infrared part of the spectrum.

That night, the block is restless. The doors are open, the phones are in heavy use, the shower teeming. Inmates take turns with the community hot pot. Some cook and others just boil water for coffee. I try the TV room, but a game of dominoes drowns out the sound. Smitty stands in the hall and observes my cellmate. Mike is outside our cell, beaming, completely unaffected by his surroundings. I approach Smitty.

"He got any grip left in his grippers?" he asks, checking my expression to make sure his thought was articulated. "I hear he was moved here from west up after someone sodomized him with a bar of soap."

I cringe. "What? Is that even possible?"

"Why are you asking me? He's your cellmate." He says the word as if the term connotes camaraderie.

"I don't know. We don't talk."

"I have to know if he's got any grip left in his grippers."

I shrug, unsure what he means. Smitty walks over to Mike. "Hey, you got any grip left in your grippers or what?" Mike just smiles. "I'm asking if you can hold in a shit or does it just fall out? Grip-in-your-grippers?"

Mike smiles even wider and turns his nose up. Smitty walks away. "What's he in for anyway?" he asks, the sarcasm gone.

"He robbed a church."

"He robbed a church? How do you rob a church?"

"He broke in after Bingo and cleaned out the lockbox."

"I thought you guys didn't talk?" Smitty looks at me suspiciously.

"We stopped after I heard he robbed a church." I shrug off the hypocrisy. My prejudice lies in the distinction between who I robbed as opposed to who, in the abstract, Mike robbed.

Smitty huffs and disappears into his cell.

Six-thirty is the time I reserved to use the phone. I move to the line and considerate inmates wrap up: *I love you, miss you, see you on Sunday.* I enter my PIN, get a dial tone, and call Mom. A recording tells me I'm being recorded. The same tells her she can permanently block me by pressing one or zero to connect.

She answers and our conversation starts out amicably: How are you? *Fine.* How is it there? *Awful.* Do you need anything? *Money for canteen?* I'll send what I can. I hate him, you know. *I know.* He destroyed the family. *I'm an adult. I could have said no.*

Could you? *I don't know.* I'd kill him if I could. *I know.* I hate him. *You already said that.* How can you not? *I'm not sure I don't.* Do you see your brother? *Sometimes, when we have movement together.* Take care of him. He idolizes your father. *I will.* We'll visit soon. okay, *Mom. I have to go.* I hang up, close to tears.

I pass Mac's cell. He's on his bunk reading. I step inside. "I notice you don't spend any time hanging out on the block."

"Bunch of chuckleheads out there. I prefer to stay away from all that bullshit." He closes the book and sets it down. His legs are crossed. The dangled foot sways left to right slowly, methodically.

"Are you guys working out tomorrow?"

"Yeah. You can work in," he answers before I can ask.

"How do you always manage to get weights?"

A half smile purses his lips. "I know the guy that cleans the weights, and he sets them aside for me before anyone gets there." Smitty storms in, asks for coffee, then storms out after he gets a scoop.

"Is he always wound so tight?" I ask after Mac settles back into exactly the same position.

"Smitty's just a troublemaker. The coffee helps him sleep"

"He just gave my cellie a ration of shit."

"For what?"

"Being gay, I guess."

"Is he?"

"It might be an insult to gay people to say he is. The dude's beyond effeminate."

Mac chuckles. "Have you seen the class board yet?"

"No."

"Where you looking to go?" he asks as if I have a say.

"I have no clue. All I know is that everyone wants to go to Norfolk and no one wants to go to Shirley."

"Trust me, they all suck. Shirley's no different from anywhere else."

"I notice that, other than Smitty, you stick to yourself?"

"Sticking to yourself is fine but still won't keep you out of trouble. It all comes down to how you handle your first situation. If someone fucks with you and you let them, then everyone will fuck with you."

"So what do I do if someone fucks with me?"

He smiles and shrugs. "If I need to tell you that, then you're in deep shit, kid."

The doors shudder, signaling count in five minutes. I make my way back to my cell, moving past Smitty's cell, where he is asleep after a full cup of coffee.

It's cold, so I fold my fire retardant blanket into a thick square and prop it where the window should be. The cop doing count barks, "Take it down."

"But there's no window," I reply. He asks if I'd like a trip to the hole for disobeying an order.

With the lights out, the cell fills with cool autumn air. It's hard to tell if the bed quakes because Mike's masturbating again or just shivering.

In prison, tobacco serves as inmate currency. Everything is paid for with smokes. You can have your laundry washed, pressed, and folded for three smokes a week and fresh fruit from a diabetic for two smokes a week. One a week gets the latest bestseller from the library.

Then the State of Massachusetts bans smoking in all prisons, citing lawsuits brought against the state brought by inmates who blame secondhand smoke for their health problems. Concord tries it first, despite rumors of riots and worker strikes, but worst of all the barter system threatens to collapse. All movement is frozen. The whole camp save the kitchen is locked down. Meals are served in the cells. Cops search the yard with metal detectors for shanks. A smoke-fest ensues twenty-four hours before all tobacco products will be considered contraband.

"You didn't smoke, did you?" I ask Mac. Smitty's answer is apparent. His jitters make a rabid chipmunk look tranquil.

"A little, but nothing that'd make me look like that. Smitty, are you going to make it, buddy?"

Smitty's frustration peaks and he blows like the cap on a steam kettle. "Fuck this, man. I need a rollie. Mac, front me some soups."

Rollies are thinned-out versions of regular cigarettes, broken up and re-rolled into three anorexic versions. Ten Ramen soups, a dollar apiece in the canteen, buys one. Get caught with one and it's a minor offense with one month loss of canteen or movement privileges, but a second offense guarantees a trip to the hole. Three offenses and they'll ship you off to Walpole, the state's only level-six maximum.

"You seriously want to pay ten bucks for a rollie you'll get three drags off of?" Mac asks Smitty.

"Fuck it. I need to smoke," Smitty pleads.

Mac gives up the soups. Smitty procures his rollie, and after three drags, it's barely a nub that singes his fingers. His eyes dart around the cell and land on the top bunk. He moves to the bed and fingers the post where a plastic cap once sealed the bed's hollow frame.

"Mac, help me tip this bunk."

Mac stares at him. "Oh no, you're not getting me lugged just so you can fish out some crusty old tobacco out of a bed frame."

"Come on, man. I'm dying."

"The beds are welded. How the fuck are you going to flip it upside down?"

Smitty shakes the frame. "Yeah, they were welded like fifty years ago. I can snap it from here."

"Dude, get out, you fucking crazy prick. I am not going to end up in the hole trying to explain how my bed became a pile of twisted metal. Go do it to your bunk."

Smitty loves Mac's suggestion and says, "Help me keep watch," to me over his shoulder. I look at Mac, who gives a disapproving nod.

I follow Smitty to his own cell, where he folds the mattresses and tosses them aside. He tries to move the frame, but it only tips as far as the opposing wall. "They must have welded the fucking things inside the cells," he mutters.

A creak and a snap later, the bunk is in pieces. He picks up one of the frames, spins and then shakes it. Debris falls out along with ash and soot. Something clinks, and Smitty shakes harder. A decomposed battery rolls out. Finally, he hits pay dirt. Several cigarette stubs roll to the floor. Most are smoked down to the nub, but a few have tobacco left on them. They're all covered in dust and some are stained with battery acid. The other frame yields several more.

"How are you going to get the bunk back together?" I ask.

"Easy. Watch and learn kid — watch and learn."

He takes off his sneakers, pulls off the laces, and ties the bed back together. The frame swings like a hammock when he tests it. "Good as new."

Smitty gets to work on rolling the pile of filth that sits on his footlocker. In all he ends up with ten rollies that he'll sell to buy fresher ones, adding that he won't charge extra for the battery acid. For a week, the block reeks with the noxious smell of tainted nicotine.

Out-Classed

I peruse the canteen list, feeling fortunate for the money to order things when people like my cellmate have to eat whatever is served in the chow hall. I order him some candy bars, coffee, and soap. The latter is more for me than him, since he doesn't seem to mind his own stench.

I offer Mike books when I finish them, but I suspect he can't read. He spends his days staring blankly at the ceiling and smirking. At night, he tosses, turns, and mumbles.

While I fill out the canteen form, I hear Smitty's door crack open. I look into the hall. Smitty is roused off his iron hammock. He slips into his prison-issue shoes. Two IPS officers come into view. One of them is clean cut, stubble outlining what was once a head of hair. The other is Latino, who is less stiff than his counterpart, with a face that looks like it is made solely of right angles but not rigid. His features are sharp, and he has piercing eyes that cast light on the whitest of lies.

Strip searches and tossing cells can happen anytime and in any part of the prison. They tell Smitty to strip down, to spread his arms, to open his mouth, to run his hands through his hair, to turn and show the bottoms of his feet, to bend and spread.

They toss him his boxers and cuff him in case he freaks out. He is told to face the wall in the hallway and not to move. "Can I put my cock back? My cock is out. Can I put it back? Better yet, can you?" Smitty asks the Latino IP.

They ignore him and pull fresh pairs of latex gloves over their hands. The Latino starts by searching every seam of Smitty's clothes, and the other pulls his bed apart and pushes the mattress into the hall. I stand frozen in the window, afraid to move, even more afraid to move away.

The IPS hit pay dirt buried inside a plastic bottle of instant iced tea. The Latino IP dumps the bottle and the fifteen rollies materialize in a puff of sugar and artificial flavoring. They place the rollies into a plastic bag and escort Smitty off the block to the hole. He smirks my way just before he disappears from view.

"Where was his cellie?" Joey asks at lunch.

"He was shipped out this morning, to Norfolk I think I heard him say," I answer.

"His cellmate ratted him out," Joey says while peeling apart his PB and J, a ritual since the bug soup. "I'd bet my dick on it."

"You think?" I ask.

"Think about it," he says, pointing to his temple. "The dude gets classed to Norfolk when everyone else is heading to Shirley. Sounds like someone ratted Smitty out to get better accommodations." His eyes shift, indicating that the conspiracy wheels are turning. Everyone in earshot braces for it. "Did you hear about the two cops from J-2 that got suspended with pay for smuggling in cartons to the runners?"

Kev nods in affirmation but offers no other details. "Five hundred a carton," Joey continues after a pause. "That's what the guards were getting, five hundred a carton. That's ten packs, twenty full sized smokes per pack broken down into three, sometimes four, rollies per smoke. That makes a pack worth $140 and a carton worth $1400, and that's why I can't get a fucking decent bag of dope, because the guards are making more money on goddamn cigarettes!"

The next day, I'm called out of the weight pit in the yard. The cop on duty hands me a pass to J-5. "Class board. Move it."

I practice my speech on the way: a good person caught up in bad circumstances, college grad, honor student, my Mom loves me. Please send me to a minimum security.

Minimums — where there is no wall, more privileges, better work assignments, more chances to earn good time — are described by everyone as country clubs. Most of the inmates I talk to say that, given my circumstances, I'm a good candidate for a minimum, all except Mac who warns me not to get my hopes up.

In J-5, the guard points me to a small office in the corner that is no bigger than a cell. In the office, a man introduces himself as my caseworker, but he never looks up from the paperwork he hunches over. The office is cramped with files, tightly bound books about Massachusetts Penal Codes, and a coffee cup that sits on several overlapping ring stains. He points to the lone chair opposite the desk. "Sit down," he says.

My body conforms to the rigid black plastic of the chair. There is a hole at my lower back, something to ooze out of when I turn into the pond scum my caseworker assumes I am.

"This is your class board. In a moment, I'll call two more of your peers into the room as witnesses. They'll each vote on where you'll end up next." His glasses sit stoutly on the bridge of his nose, which is too small for his face. His polo shirt is the color of watermelon, not a fresh version but the chemically concocted combination of red #40 and blue lake #5. "Sign here saying that you have agreed to participate in the proceedings. You can read, can't you?" he asks. It's the first time he looks at me.

"Yes," I reply.

"Where do you want to go?" he asks, shuffling papers around.

"I was hoping to go to a minimum."

He peers at me over the rim of his glasses. The only one of my rights I can remember is the one about remaining silent. Nine words in and I've already blown it.

"You're W55906, right?" he asks, scanning the file as if he missed something.

"That's my con number, yes."

"And which minimum did you want to be sent to?"

"Middleton is probably the closest for my mother and grandmother to visit."

His head bobbles from side to side. "I don't think so." He gathers my paperwork and walks out, file in hand.

He returns with two guards. One of them is Rock and the other is a pimple-faced kid whose trepidation nearly overrides mine. He looks as if strings were pulled to get him the job. Unlike Rock, who looks as if he was bred specifically for this line of work. My caseworker sits, then gives me the once over as if it's the first time he's set eyes on me. "What have you done since you got here?"

"What have I done about what?" I reply.

"What have you done to rehabilitate yourself?" His tone is subdued.

"Rehabilitate?" I ask. "I wasn't aware that I was supposed to be rehabilitating."

"You're not working?" the caseworker asks.

"No, but…"

"Have you involved yourself in any programs?" he interrupts.

"No."

The caseworker leans back after lifting his coffee cup, revealing a new moist ring. "So you're not working and you haven't attended any programs? How about church? Do you go to church?"

Rock sniffles, more like a snort, and snarls.

"No, I don't go to church," I answer.

My caseworker asks me to leave so that they can confer. Less than five minutes later, I'm called back and informed that they unanimously decided to send me to Shirley, not a minimum by any measure.

I spend most of the night looking at the steel pole outside, atop which sits a lamp powerful enough to illuminate half the yard. An array of moths flutter in a dizzying display of acrobatics, each taking turns crashing into the glass shield that protects the bulb. One of them crashes into the screen, lodging one of its legs into the tightly woven squares. It struggles, panics, stops moving, then panics again and twitches about like mad. I watch with empathy, familiar with his struggle, but I do not free him. It would take an effortless flick of my finger to set him free, but he's the most entertainment I've had during these sleepless nights, and so I abstain from being this creature's salvation.

I reach into my locker for my legal pad and pen and sift through the seven written pages of the letter I started to Dad, anxious to send it off before his court date and inevitable arrival.

Weaponized Chicken of the Sea

Shirley is heralded as the worst prison in the system, the reputation gained after a riot in 1995. Inmates trapped guards in a stairwell for just under an hour, until shotgun blasts and teargas dispersed the inciters. Officials blamed the overcrowding. Carl was there and said it was a result of a guard with a chip on his shoulder harassing a lifer with an even bigger one.

"It was pandemonium for a few minutes, but the whole thing was a joke." Carl shrugs it off. Carl is a runner on the block, an old-timer with five bids under his belt and a deceptively short fuse. He copes with day-to-day frustrations with ease, yet threatens to stab me in the neck if I throw one more deuce during a game of spades. Last time he was out, he only made it twenty-four hours before bludgeoning someone until they were unidentifiable.

"What really sucked is that, afterwards, we were locked down for three days. The State Police came in and searched every cell. They looked for anyone who would rat. If you gave them a name they didn't smash your TV. They smashed mine." He laughs.

"Shirley is like anywhere else. You keep to yourself. Don't get caught up in anything stupid. Do your time. You'll be fine." Mac puts me at ease as I sit on his footlocker.

He looks briefly as if he's searching for something soothing to say but remains silent and stares out the window. Finally he says, "This last time out I was running dope for a friend. I was making great money and refused to get high. I even had a girlfriend and an old MG, used but in good shape, a convertible." His eyes thin to a slit as he stares into the past. I'm unsure if he's talking to me or to the wall.

"A good friend of mine was managing a Stop and Shop Supermarket," he continues. "You know, the ones where the offices are perched in lofts in the front corner of the store? I'd meet him there and you could look out at the whole store, and what you couldn't see, the closed circuit cameras picked up." He uncrosses and crosses his legs. Mike floats by the door on his way to the shower. An argument brews over one of the phones.

"This buddy of mine fronted some dope, a lot actually. He was one of those casual users that thought they could sell it and just use the profits. I didn't have the heart to tell him that never works." He sips his coffee. Steam billows from the rim and dissipates. The aroma reaches me and strikes at something familiar, reminiscent. "It was around that time that my mother died from a massive stroke. My dad thought it might be a good time to tell me I was adopted, which blew my mind. My real parents were Native Americans. I came straight off the reservation." He looked at me and saw that I was studying him intently. "Yeah, I know what you're thinking. Hispanic, right?"

I want to justify my prejudice, but it was useless. Mac closes his eyes briefly as if delivering absolution in a quick decisive gesture, and then he continues, "It freaked me out more than I thought it would. I had no idea. My parents were Hispanic so there was a resemblance. It wasn't like they were blonde and blue eyed. That news messed me up bad I think because I started shooting dope that night. It didn't take long before I was dipping into the product I was supposed to be delivering. This shit was dealer-to-dealer stuff, very potent, and I was stepping all over it. The dealers in question caught on and I ended up staring down the barrel of a shotgun while some Dominican screamed for his money. He figured I owed him ten grand, considering how much I was dipping in at the end. I didn't argue."

Mac delivers this soliloquy languidly, his face cloaked in the shadow of the bed frame, his cellmate's blanket untucked and hanging. "I drove that MG, Jesus, must've been a buck fifty to that Stop and Shop. I parked outside the range of the parking lot cameras, slid in a side entrance while some kid was on a smoke break. I knew if my buddy saw me on the cameras, he'd jet. He was up in his office, and I surprised the shit out of him." He reaches in his shirt pocket and pulls out a smoke, not a rollie but an actual brand name cigarette.

"You're smoking now? Hell of a time to start." I close one eye, expecting the smoke to sting quickly in such close quarters.

He snickers. "It's funny with me, you know? I can smoke this and ten more and just stop. That's how it's always been, even with dope — I can just quit." The cigarette cinched between his thumb and forefinger, Mac blows smoke out of the corner of his mouth toward the open window.

"I caught him getting the nightly deposit ready to drop off. The safe behind him was open and I could see stacks of cash. I sat down, casual, and waited. He told me he was too busy to talk, that I should have called him first. And worst of all, he said he didn't have my money. To top it all off, he had a dog shit attitude about it. So I snapped." He paused and waited for me to ask.

"So what'd you do?"

"I walked around his desk, grabbed him by the throat, and just started wailing on him. He was out cold by the time I finished. So I grabbed a plastic bag, you know the ones they put your groceries in, and emptied the safe. I only intended on taking what he owed me, but then I thought, fuck it, may as well take it all. I took the cash, checks, and credit card receipts. I even took a few rolls of change until it weighted down the bag too much. On my way out I reached over a cashier and grabbed a carton of smokes. Her eyes nearly popped out when she saw my bloody knuckles. I think it tipped her off to what I had just done because she screamed."

"So how much was in the bag?"

"Thirty thou in cash."

"So you paid the Dominican guy?"

"Plus I bought a ton of dope. I picked up my girl and hightailed it to a hotel. We spent two weeks getting fucked up before the cops found the MG parked outside and busted in. She turned State's evidence."

"That sucks."

"Nah, not really. She didn't deserve all that trouble," he says quietly. I noted the stark difference to the usual inference that the woman along for the ride should have kept quiet, that her character was marred by the act of pointing a finger to save herself.

The doors crack: count is in five. I stand and stretch, procrastinate about the walk back to my cell and the sleepless night that lies ahead, then make my way to my bunk. After count, I fill out my canteen list to drop off as I pick up the previous week's order. Mike has come to expect his candy and soap and I enjoy making him think I forgot.

The next morning, Ritchie, the block's runner, looks around the cell before his eyes settle on me, staring briefly. Before I can ask, he shoves something under the door and disappears.

Mike stirs but flops back to his previous position after he sees it's only a newspaper. I twist myself around and reach for it without leaving the bunk. I open it to reveal my father on the front page, his elbows propped on the arms of a chair, fingers interlaced and supporting his chin. Handcuffs peek out from under his shirt. The suit he wears no longer portrays the tenacious salesman it once draped. A bailiff stands behind him trying to look ominous. The headline reads: "Mastermind of Father-Son Jewel Heist Team Jailed."

My dad stares. I know he's not looking at the judge. His face is softer. He's bald, the last strands that connected ear to ear now shaved. There are no signs of stress, just a cold stare.

As I scan the article, words jump out at me: *mastermind, stole two million, victims live in fear, showed no emotion, twelve years in prison.* I focus on what the judge says before he orders Dad loaded into a van and driven to Concord.

This concludes a bizarre series of crimes that I am still unable to fully understand. It is really quite extraordinary, and very, very sad. How, as a father, you could have involved your sons in this is beyond my capacity as a father to comprehend. But we all have choices in this world. And you are going to live with yours for a long time.

The article concludes that, during a robbery, my father threatened the victim's life if he didn't report that the robbery was committed by three African Americans.

"Canteen, A through M, pickup," the sergeant yells.

The doors open. I'm aware of everyone black on the block, especially Malakai and his cellmate Donovan. I know from Mac that they are both gang affiliated.

Malakai mills about the block when the call comes for N through Z to pickup canteen. I slip on my bobos and dart out the door.

"He's here?" I ask Kev as we wait in line to pick up our packages.

"At intake, probably going to J-1."

"Did you read the article?" I whisper.

His shoulders slump. "No, what article? Another one? Jesus Christ!"

"With his picture and everything. Remember what we told that dude at the end of the Burlington robbery?"

"No," he answers after a look of pain passes.

I whisper through gritted teeth, "Three black guys?"

"Big deal," he says.

I snatch my bags without checking the order and hurry back to the block and the safety of the cell, mindful of every look cast upon me, feeling in their gaze the justification to smite me down for my insolence.

Back on the block, I scurry toward my cell, the length of the hall eternal. Donovan is near the phones. I'm the first one back from group N through Z. Those in A through M are busy unpacking their things. The less fortunate scuttle around the block hoping for handouts.

Malakai emerges from his cell and limps toward me. I drift to the opposite side of the hallway to avoid him. He adjusts and meets me head-on.

"Excuse me," I say and move to sidestep his intrusion into my proverbial space.

"Where you going with my canteen, white boy?" His breath smells of corn chips. I avoid eye contact.

"Excuse me?" My knees feel like they might buckle.

"My canteen," Malakai says.

"Our canteen," Donovan reiterates over my shoulder. I feel his humidity. "As a matter of fact, you can drop that shit off every week from now on, white boy."

Deadlocks clank. The door that connects the east and west sides of the building creaks. The sergeant emerges, keys jingling from his belt.

"Listen dude, I don't want any trouble. You can have the bags. Just let me bring them to my cell so the sergeant doesn't suspect anything. When he's gone, you can have them."

"Do that," he responds.

I walk back to my cell. Mike's putrid feet hang like dirty ham hocks. I set the bags down, shaking uncontrollably.

Mike sits up and rubs the sleep from his eyes. I pull a pair of socks from my locker and stuff one into the other, then fill them with tuna cans. The sock top wraps around my wrist and turns my skin white. I grip the slack. The cans feel alive as they tap against my leg.

Donovan tries to shout out a warning, but surprise stays on my side. I aim to take out Malakai first. I wind with a backhand. The cans crash against the side of his head and he's down in an instant.

I turn my sights on Donovan, and simultaneously the call goes out. The sergeant shouts into the receiver clipped to his shoulder, "Move team to east down! I repeat, move team to east down!"

Somewhere I know officers are suiting up, preparing to take me by force. The weight of the cans pulls my arm across my body. I wield the makeshift mace and aim for the porous flesh of Donovan's shoulder, but he turns to avoid the blow and takes it in the chest. I swing them circular, gain momentum, and bring the cans down on his head.

Those who know are already on the floor, waiting. I foresee the disciplinary committee suspecting a hate crime, and so I turn my mace on Ritchie, the closest Caucasian. The shaking subsides. I kneel at the sergeant's behest, interlace my fingers behind my head, and lay on my stomach per his demands.

By the time the other officers reach the block, I am down, voluntarily in the position they usually have to forcibly bend someone into. They shackle me wrist to ankle and escort me off the block. I have to find the right number of short steps that'll keep me in line with their march. The guard on my left clamps down on my arm with a thick gloved hand and yanks me off my pace. A plastic bag marked evidence swings from his other clutched fist. Tuna cans threaten to breach the plastic and stretch the letters in EVIDENCE to circus mirror proportions. Eyes are on me. I cause a lockdown. All movement ceases until I'm subdued.

The guard in the Seg Unit stands next to an open cell halfway down the hall. I'm led inside and told to kneel while they take off the leg irons. They leave the handcuffs on and close the door. A rectangle flap in the door is jarred open, and a voice beckons for me to back into the door and place my hands through the space. It's a hard angle, and my wrists scrape on the rigid edges. The cuffs are removed, and I feel the flap close against my fingers as a warning that the small space is being shut.

I wring my wrists, trying to ease the sting, and take in my surroundings. With the flap shut, the only light is from a bulb confined by a hard plastic shroud bolted to the ceiling and cradled by an iron grate. The room is empty except for a thin pad on top of a concrete slab and a toilet/sink combo. Everything is deep storm-cloud gray. I push myself into the corner and ball up, exhausted. My hands cup my face just before my stomach heaves deep bellied sobs into my throat. I try to squelch them so they can't be heard.

I am chilled by the cold concrete but fall asleep in the fetal position. Slumber takes me by force and projects spliced scenes from my life onto the back of my skull, again in full sensory overload. My mind conjures the smell of mist slowly burning off the lake that Mom took us to every year. Toast burns in the distant kitchen of the restaurant and triggers an insatiable hunger, which manages to transmute to lust as my first love, Ellen, steps closer. The smell of her perfume sparks the fire that consumes all reason and leaves only impulse. Then comes gluttony, as my last high plays out in Technicolor. A bent spoon full of cocaine sits level on the sink ledge, a solid white chunk next to it, another on the steel wool of the glass stem and melting under the flame of the lighter. Smoke fills my lungs. My heartbeat becomes a stomp.

I awake to the sound of the door opening. A pool of drool sits like mercury on the painted concrete. My face is indented from the folds of my shirt pressing into my flesh. Two IPS officers enter the cell. One fills the threshold while the other ducks passively, as if the ceiling is too low. The one in the door is as wide as he is tall. The other is pointed, with a narrow head, long nose, and deep-set, piercing eyes. Red freckles speckle his powdery white skin. I immediately mistrust of him, which puts my back up. I know what this visit is because Mac told me about it.

The one in the door folds his arms across his chest. The muscles of his forearms overlap. He leans, and the act seems too timed, initiated in sync with the other one leaning forward and attending to me, maybe the body language taught to guards by retired lion tamers.

"We're just here to try to ascertain what happened," the pointy one says in an even tone devoid of emotion. These assholes all use words like ascertain, incident, and code so-and-so in zone here-or-there.

I clam up, heeding Mac's past advice.

"Do you want to tell us what happened?" Pointy snickers and tilts his head with a half shrug, gesturing that if he was in my position he'd have more to say. The wide one shifts in the doorway and places his hands in his pockets. I shake my head no.

The pointy one sits back as if my refusal is a setback in guard/convict relations. He readjusts. A slight crane in his neck indicates a change in tactics. "Looks pretty bad, you beating down those three guys. You could get more time for assault and battery with a dangerous weapon." He smirks as if he relates. "I'd hate to see that. Sergeant says you're quiet, and he even went so far as to comment that he wishes he had a whole block of your type: quiet, stick-to-yourself. He said he just can't figure why you'd fly off like that." He stares off and I imagine he is scanning his hidden agenda. "Unless maybe you were being strong-armed?"

Then I violate the first law of the poker face — never let your eyes give you away. I stare somewhere between his rat face and the human blockade's boots when his question forces me to lock eyes with him. Part of me wants to talk, but I can see Mac's nodding apparition behind them. Even a short conversation about the facts will be viewed as ratting to those within earshot. The fact of the matter is that just these officers' presence in the cell will be enough to brand me with that label. I know my only strategy must be silence.

When it's clear I won't talk, the pointy one turns to his partner and says, "This'll be an easy report to write."

The wide one steps back to let his partner out of the cell. He keeps his eyes on me as the door closes, more to watch for second thoughts I think than because he is worried about a potential attack. I curl back up and the light switches off. There's a sliver of faint light filling the space under the door, barely enough to outline the contours of the toilet. My stomach roars and I rampantly search for something to focus on that'll distract me from the worry that threatens to overwhelm me. Blackness moves in waves as if my eyes can detect dark's war on the light. I think of a candle, how it radiates outward, pulsing, pushing light as far is it is able, fighting the darkness that threatens to snuff it out. I think of the flame, how it breathes, consumes, reproduces, but dies if deprived of the necessary fuel to keep it alive.

The disciplinary committee members sit slumped over the folding table of the nondescript room, a tribunal of stuffed suits. Papers are shuffled. One-word discussions take place over breath scented with stale coffee and the previous night's microwave dinner. If this is a collection of my peers, I have a hard time making the connection that would qualify them. Their jowls wag. There are no introductions.

It's possible they're expert penologists, degreed and certified to render judgment. But it's more likely that I am in the presence of four soon-to-be retired pencil pushers empowered to decide my fate based on a whim or the facts, whichever suits their fancy.

The middle committee member addresses me while the rest stare into space. They decide that I am to return to population with a sixty day suspension of canteen privileges and no movement for the remainder of the month.

My first stop on the block is Mac's cell, but he's at work. My cell door is open. Mike is packing. "Where are you headed?" I ask.

"Gardner," he says, not bothering to look up from his packing. He's putting a lot of thought into the placement of his scant possessions that'll end up getting tossed into the back of a transport van anyway.

He takes the last of his candy bars from his locker, one he savored and rationed so it would last until I bought him another. He turns and shoves it at me without making eye contact. The gesture nearly bowls him over.

"No, Mike. You take it, although it'll be tough to eat while you're shackled in the back of the van. Maybe you should eat it now. I smelled fish on my way back to the block."

Mike takes my advice, tears the wrapping, and shoves the candy bar into his mouth. When he is packed, he floats down the hallway without a word, dribbling chocolate onto his prison-issue shirt.

With the door closed, I realize that the J's are in the yard. I scan the faces that pass my window as the prisoners aimlessly walk the track. I recognize him from farther away than my eyes can focus, recognize him based on a lifetime of witnessing the nuances of his walk, the straightness of his spine, the gleam off his bald head. It was him, no doubt about it.

I duck under the window frame and raise up enough to bring him back into view, Dad alive and in person. I remember the day Kev and I pled guilty. That was as close to him as I had been in over a year.

He looks no different now than he did that day. The heavy denim seems tailor made, as if Dad visited a different intake window, one equipped with an Italian seamstress who chalk marked his denim and tacked it accordingly. I find it strange, as I squat, half straddling my locker, that he doesn't look as out of place as my mind's eye projected. As a matter of fact, he looks right at home, strolling along the track with another older gentleman like two retirees in search of a pond full of ducks to befriend.

At lunch, my brother thumps the table. "That was stupid," he concludes with no invitation to explain. "And what if they lugged you out of here? You should've thought about Mom and what having to visit two different prisons would do to her," he barks.

I shrug. There is no outcome he would have approved of. "Won't Mom have to do that anyway when I go to Shirley?"

The look on his face says my brother fails to appreciate my logic when I tell him the same scenario exists for Mom whether I slung tuna cans or not. So, I change the subject. "I have no cellmate now. Is there a way to request that you come over to east down?"

"Go see the assignment officer after you eat," Joey interjects.

The superintendent, housing officer, and work detail officer all stand outside the chow hall so that inmates wishing to bring up issues can approach them. The housing officer's mirrored sunglasses conceal eyes that I'm sure never set on me. His chin dips to affirm that I'm more than a nagging voice in his head, and he shakes his head no. I persist with more heartfelt reasons for the coupling. He threatens me with a trip to the hole.

I return to my cell and stare out into the yard. Kev's face fills the window of the door. "Are you coming in here?" I am worried because my door hasn't cracked.

"Next door," he answers.

"Lock in," the amplified voice of the guard bellows from the other end of the block.

"I'll see you at movement," I say.

I lie back down and drift, every pore reacting to the heat. Sunlight blazes the cell and pushes against my eyelids. Dad's voice calls through the haze. I answer from a dream. He searches for me, pulls me out of the blinding light and eclipses it, sheltering me so that I can see him clearly. My fears vanish. He gathers me and I feel his remorse in the strength of his hug, which envelops me until I wake, disappointed. Dad calls my name from the yard, keeping his distance from the fence and acting inconspicuous. If the guards catch him yelling through the fence, he'll get lugged.

"Hey Dad," I answer.

"Dad, what block are you on?" Kev interrupts.

"I'm in J-1. How are you guys holding up?"

"Good," my brother answers. I repeat it.

"Dad, try to get assigned to east down. Talk to the assignment officer at lunch tomorrow," Kev yells.

"I have a friend in the kitchen and he's going to try to get me into the Mods."

The Mods house the permanent work force. It doesn't surprise me that Dad's made connections.

Despite the turmoil on the block, everyone milling about, vocal chords straining after lying dormant for a long time, news of Nutsy's presence among us travels the grapevine of inmates standing idle. The news comes to a dead stop at my cell.

"Not Nutsy. Dude, I'm sorry." Kev offers condolence before I even know what a Nutsy is.

The crowd parts, but not in honor or fear — to make room for Nutsy's enormity. He wears depravity's uniform, fat, but he is clearly not the victim of an underactive thyroid. The man eats. Every part of him consumes, from the space he takes up to the air he sucks in with a wheeze. His round black eyes swallow his surroundings, constantly searching for what might be edible, smokable, fuckable.

"Where am I?" His gargling phlegm-filled voice sounds like feet walking on gravel. "This the one?" He peers around me, past my ploy to block the numbers on the door. "Yeah, yeah, this is it."

He drags two full laundry bags behind him. His stomach, one giant mound of viscera covered with fat, tests the tensile strength of his shirt and pants. Once we lock in, he moves sloppily around the cell and places things inside his locker.

"Eh, you know my knees are bad and my back hurts." He pauses and gums at the unglued dentures swimming around his mouth. "Maybe you could give me the bottom?"

"Maybe not," I answer rudely.

Nutsy grabs hold of the crossbar. I expect a drop in cabin pressure when he inhales. His belly sways. His tree trunk thigh lifts to gain footing. Success brings a quake that threatens to telescope the bed frame and reduce it to a pile of twisted metal. Springs stretch to their limit once he's up. I'm left staring at the receiving end of the indentation caused by his girth. Each adjustment he makes causes aftershocks that increase my fear of being crushed.

"Eh, do we eat early or late around here?" he grunts.

"When the door opens, we eat," I respond.

"Eh, you got any food? You get canteen?"

I ignore him. He grunts something only he understands. I read but can't ignore the fact that quiet to Nutsy is two decibels above noisy.

And as if I didn't have enough to contend with trying to coax sleep into my combatant brain, the coup de grace to my attempt at sleep is Nutsy's snore, which is more than the product of a deviated septum. It's a roar cursing Mother Nature, pleading with her to rewrite the rules of fornication if only to avoid another genetic mishap like the one above me.

The next day Nutsy dives for the mail as soon as it's shoved under the door and stands looking dumbfounded by the letter he holds. I wait, sure he'll let me in on what puzzles him so.

"Nutsy, what's up?" I ask finally when all he does is stare at the envelope.

"Eh, this letter I wrote to my buddy came back to me. It says return to sender, addressee decreased." He turns it over. "Decreased, what the hell is decreased?"

"Let me see." I sit up and snatch the letter from his hands. "Nutsy, it says deceased, not de-creased."

"Eh, what's deceased?" he asks.

"He's dead, Nutsy."

"Dead? What do you mean dead?"

For a split second, I think he means the question in a metaphysical sense, like what does it truly mean to be dead? Then I remember that Nutsy spends his days drawing trucks and coloring them in. "He's dead, has died, is no more, passed away." I run out of synonyms. He huffs and throws the letter away in the trash.

"Son?" Dad calls through the fence.

"Eh, your Dad's calling you. He's right here! Hold on!" Nutsy yells.

"I can hear him, Nutsy! Shut up!" I yell back, and I hear my brother chuckle, obviously getting a kick from my woes as usual.

"Hey Dad," I call out.

"I think we have movement together tomorrow. Come to the yard. I'll meet you there," my father yells, and then he leaves without waiting for an answer.

"You took my advice a little literally don't you think?" Mac asks as we walk together toward the yard, referring to the tuna incident.

"You said to handle my first situation, so I handled it," I say bluntly, in no mood to joke around.

"I said handle it, not throttle the shit out of your assailants. Anyway, I'd probably have done the same." He smirks, but I can tell he sees me in a different light, an unexpected light.

"Do you think anyone will retaliate?" I ask.

"Nah. Those guys are just hustlers. Anyone important wouldn't be hustling you for canteen. Besides, they shipped those clowns out of here the day it happened. As far as I know, they're in Walpole," he said, breaking off from our course and heading toward the property building. "See ya later, kid. I'm off to work. You set on sheets and shit?"

I nod yes, my eyes focused on Dad waiting for me in the yard ahead. He looks taller than ever. I check the proportions, his height to that of the wall, and it looks like they are close to the same height, but somehow the wall looks dwarfed. Dad gathers me in, pulls me close, and hugs me. It feels uncomfortable. Eyes are on us.

"Boy, it's been so long since I've seen you without either a few inches of glass or a fence between us. How are you doing, son?" He releases me. I step back and start walking, needing to move.

"I'm doing good, Dad. How about you?" I ask, wondering why he didn't open with the letter, at least some mention of its contents. If I had a son and he wrote me the letter I wrote to him, I'd have trouble mentioning anything but. I'd spend the rest of my life trying to help him understand, to ease the distress apparent in every written word.

It's not like I wrote the letter in code. I let him off the hook in that respect. He didn't have to read between the lines — it was all spelled out. I refuse to let him off the hook again. If he blows it off, so be it.

"I'm doing fine, son. Just settling in."

"It's been a long road, eh?" I ask, silently damning myself for bringing up the topic before he does.

"A greater understatement has never been uttered, I'm afraid," he replies.

As we complete a lap, I talk myself down and formulate excuses for him. Broaching your son's contempt can't be easy, I tell myself.

"What was your Dad like?" I ask him.

"My father? Why do you ask about him?" he asks in an accusatory tone, as if he's cracked the code before I can spell out all the clues.

"No reason. It's just that I've never heard you talk about him."

"There's not much to tell. He was a mechanic. He worked hard. He fixed planes during World War One. He died young." He rattles off these particulars as if he's dictating his father's obituary to a scribe.

"Were you close?" I ask.

"Not really," he replies.

"And Uncle Dennis, were you close to him?" I ask.

"We were ten years apart," he replies.

"And Grandma, were you close to her?"

"More now than then."

"Mom says you used to hit her. Any truth to that?" I ask.

"None," he replies.

"Why would she lie?" I ask.

"I couldn't even attempt a guess. Your Mom drank a lot, and her mother hated me."

I have no clue how many laps we complete in the process of this little talk. Finally, I throw my knuckleball. "Dad, you just got hit with twelve years in prison. Twelve years. How do you feel about that? I mean, it's almost a life sentence."

We stop. "Son…" He takes a deep, labored breath. "I've had a full life. I've traveled, seen most of the world, the parts I wanted to see anyway. I took your grandmother to Hawaii. I've been married, twice. I was successful according to most measurements. I had a great job, a decent career, owned two houses. Honestly, I really don't regret anything."

Our time is up. Inmates filter out. I feel like an innocent bystander after some conman pulls the old sleight of hand routine and, instead of picking the same card you picked from the deck, he lifts your wallet.

Sociopathic Tendencies

Nutsy is snoring. He is not asleep, but he is snoring just the same. I'm waiting for the call to the visiting room. It's Thanksgiving and we're expecting Mom and Grandma. Holidays sting. A gray melancholic cloud hangs low over the prison.

The entire prison is somber. Except for count, the doors are left open. The smell of turkey floats on the light fog that curtails a flock of geese from their southerly flight. They're in the yard, waddling around and scavenging for bugs. I watch them steer clear of our block and the ungodly bellow of Nutsy's snore that staves off all living things.

Nutsy anxiously awaits dinner, which is rumored to be fresh turkey and not turkey roll — lips and assholes and organ meat pressed into a loaf and sliced up several times a week. "Eh, last year there was mashed potatoes and gravy with stuffing," Nutsy says while rubbing his tummy. I wonder where his body will store any more fat. Every morning I expect to wake to two Nutsy's after his body is forced into mitosis and splits. One of them would continue to roam in search of more food. Then I think that this has already happened, and this Nutsy *is* the latter half.

At count, the doors close and Nutsy dresses. He pulls out his prison-issue button down still creased from being stuffed in the bottom of his locker. He brushes what's left of his hair. A wad of it ends up tangled in the bristles. He primps as if preparing for a date, one that he'll schmooze, charm, caress, then devour. In fact, Nutsy talks to his food and hums while he chews. No one has ever gotten close enough to ascertain what he says.

When he's done, he stands at the door, which remains closed for count, and the eventual call to dinner. He nervously paces at the threshold. He listens carefully to what block is called next. He gives me updates: "Eh, J-2. They called J-2."

At last, the moment arrives and the doors crack. But Nutsy is overanxious and tries to slip out the door before its open enough to fit his bloated frame. He gets stuck when the door shorts out and jams. Nutsy snaps.

"Open the fucking door!" Nutsy convulses. "Hey! Open the fucking door!" My brother tries not to laugh, and in fact, he tries to calm Nutsy. Nutsy only sees his chances at the first tray of piping-hot turkey dwindle. "Two forty-two! Open fucking two forty-two!"

The sergeant ignores the urgency in Nutsy's profanity and looks over the problem. Maintenance is called, and ten minutes later, the repair person jars open the door and Nutsy is freed. He bolts to the chow hall.

After dinner, the call comes in. The guard calls my brother and me after cracking our doors. I've been ready for over an hour.

My brother is just pulling on his pants and seems surprised by the interruption into his third nap of the day.

Mom visits almost every week. I try to keep her laughing because it's better than the alternative: sitting listlessly and aching over the past. All visits are "contact." Inmates sit next to their loved ones and are allowed one hug at the beginning and one at the end. The kissing of a significant other is allowed but only closed mouthed — it says as much on the sign that also includes strict rules about passing anything that might be considered contraband to the inmate, drugs especially. Every rule seems to defy common sense by stating the obvious, even insulting common sense. The walls are also decorated with the Massachusetts General Law that spells out the penalty for violating the rules: three years in prison and a hundred thousand dollar fine.

"That bitch out front makes me take off my wig every week. She does it every week. I'm eighty-seven years old. What the hell am I going to put in my wig?" my grandmother states at the beginning of every visit, and then she launches into a lengthy address on how the system screwed us. She and Dad sit next to each other. Kev sits next to Dad and I sit next to Mom. Mom picks the furthest point away from Dad and whispers, "If I get close enough, I'll tear his heart out."

Mom spends most of her time during the visit talking about her newfound religion, Wicca. "It's so wonderful. It's an earth-based religion that celebrates polytheism. That's the belief in more than one god," she adds.

"I know, Mum," I reply, robbing her of her chance to enlighten me.

"Isn't that witchcraft?" my brother interjects as his eyebrows slope downward. He is perplexed.

"Yeah, but it's so cool." Her face brightens, and a few of the deeper wrinkles seem to fade momentarily as her lips turn upward into a smile. "The Catholics hate us. Would you believe they caused such a ruckus over the festival the church planned? They came to the field where it was held just so they could bless it before we heathens showed up?"

"That's fantastic, Mum," I say.

"It's all bullshit," my brother says, adding a dose of his own religion, pessimism.

"All bullshit? Why do you say that?" my mother asks.

"There is no God," he says.

I roll my eyes and prepare myself for a drawn out self-pity session. "Don't say that, sweetie. I know it's hard not to think of things like that in here, but when you get out, you'll start over, fresh." Mom sounds so optimistic, but she makes a calculated mistake. She mentions the only two words that remind us of how many more days, minutes, and seconds we have left in our sentence, a number that is much more calculable for me than it is for Kev.

"I'm never getting out of here," he says. I think that, at about this point, Mom realizes that she'll have to learn a whole new language, a more tactful set of words, omitting the one she's used to using. In particular, I assume she crossed off this set of words on her list today — when you get out.

"I don't blame you for feeling that way, but there is an end to this — there has to be. That's all I can think about. It's the only way I can survive." She slides her arm around Kev, rousing the attention of the guard standing at the end of the row of chairs.

"And what the hell am I supposed to do then, with felonies on my record?"

I back off to let him stew, but Mom looks to me for help. "Thanks to him, I almost got sent to the hole for getting my hair cut," I say.

"How'd he do that?" she asks and obviously welcomes the change of subject.

My brother smirks and answers before I do. "It takes frigging six weeks to get called for a haircut in the barbershop, which is across the hall from canteen, and so I told him to walk in after he picked up his order."

"More like shoved me in and ordered them to cut it," I interject.

"Whatever." My brother reverts to the tried and true defense he uses whenever someone points out his bullishly antisocial attitude. It's one of the major tenants of pessimism: I did it, it was wrong, whatever.

"And your little plan would have worked, if it weren't for the guard who came in two seconds after you left and freaked out on me," I say.

"What'd you do?" Mom asks, wide eyed and worried.

"He asked me who the hell I was. I didn't know what to say so I got philosophical on him. I said, 'Does anyone really *know* who they are?'" Kev and Mom both crack up laughing, asking me to confirm and reconfirm my audacity.

"You did not say that. Did you?" Mom asks. My brother can hardly breathe.

It never happened. I just needed to get them laughing again. While they are keeled over, Dad reaches over Grandma and taps me on the shoulder. "What's so funny?"

"Me, I guess," I answer.

"But you're not funny," he says, four tiny words the equivalent of three quick jabs to the heart. I try to ignore his comment but it sits on my chest and constricts my ability to breathe. "Oh, and son," he adds like a ninja passing unseen, leaving only a dead body as evidence he was ever there. "I got your letter and look forward to discussing it sometime."

Shackled and Shipped to Shirley

I wait for a visit. Mom's coming with Grandma. The anticipation weighs me down. I'm worried because Mom coughed up blood last week and she's waiting for word from her doctor.

My door cracks. I walk out and notice Kev's remains closed. Sometimes two separate calls come in, a sign of the prison's inefficiency. I expect to be handed a pass. Instead, the guard looks at his clipboard, follows the list of con numbers sent to him from transport, and says, "Pack it up. You're out of here."

Ironically, all I can think of is Nutsy, how I won't be listening to him snore tonight. I decide that I'll leave what's left of my canteen to my brother so I can cheat my cellie out of a meal — hell on earth to Nutsy.

"What's up?" Kev asks from his window.

"Shirley. Today," I answer just as his door cracks and he's called for a visit. "Tell Mum." I start stuffing things into my fishnet sack. Nutsy is roused. Pavlov's dog hears the bag of oatmeal cookies crinkle as I pack.

"That sucks," Kev adds. The guard calls him again, and Kev hugs me for the first time in our lives, a quick and uncomfortable hug.

"Eh, where you going?" Nutsy digs goop from the corners of his eyes and wipes it on his shirt.

"Shirley, Nutsy. Here, before you go, take the rest of my canteen," I say to my brother as I hand it to him.

One pack of chocolate pop tarts, the cookies that woke Nutsy, toiletries, a few cans of tuna. Nutsy watches the bag change hands. I know he's salivating. He climbs down, ready to take over the bottom bunk. It's a rite of passage. His next cellmate will have to eat crow and take the top unless he has a typewritten letter from the prison doctor stating he has claustrophobia, a bum hip, or a bad knee. But letters like that are mostly ignored anyway.

Nothing on my pass to transport is legible except my con number. Transport is a slew of scurrying guards because no one knows who's shipping out until the very last minute. The driver of the transport van is armed, entrusted with the distinct task of passing us through the free world unnoticed.

I'm placed in a wire mesh cage, and a guard plops a duffle bag down near the door. Con numbers are called, one by one. Each inmate is shackled, wrist to waist, waist to ankle, ankle to ankle. When it is my turn, I step out, kneel, stand, and turn as the guard decorates me in chrome. My wrists are heavy and the steel limits my range of motion. Scratching requires a yoga master's litheness.

The van is packed tight with prisoners, and there is no personal space on the hard wooden benches. Turns in the road pose the risk of unwanted intimacy. No one showered first, and I would swear that some of these guys have never showered. The van pulls out of the bay. We stop in a trap. The gate to the outside is impossible to open if the gate behind is ajar. Guards holding mirrors attached to long poles flank each side. The underside of the van is searched for stowaways as the guard in the tower above watches intently.

The world outside looks different, clearer, and unbound, like being pulled from a fish tank as my perception shifts from the reality of inside. The van pulls into a Dunkin Donuts, enacting the simplicity of daily life I took for granted. I hear them order: two medium coffees, one regular, one with milk and Splenda, a bagel sandwich.

The ride down Route 2 is quiet except for the guards' voices raised over the hum of the engine, the wind of the transmission. The guards settle into a pattern: sip, chat, laugh. The one on the right savors his sandwich, biting every third sip, holding it gingerly in his hand, cupped by his palm. Only the occasional call over the radio breaks the steadiness of their rhythm.

We pull off the highway. Gardner is ahead. Only one of us was actually classed here, but when we stop and the light of the setting sun floods the back of the van, it's announced that everyone is getting out but me.

Back on the highway I try to relish the surroundings. With the back empty, I can see out the windshield. Winter coats both sides of the highway, and the guardrail comes to life, twisting into the long and unknown ahead, moving rapidly head on, repetitious and blurred behind when I look out the back window.

Concord was set up like a cemetery, the oldest buildings like century-old headstones. Every sharp angle was eroded long ago, smoothed by the slow passage of time. Stouter, state-of-the-art structures dwarf the old ones, the combination of past and present thrown together seemingly haphazardly.

Shirley isn't surrounded by a sixty foot concrete wall. Instead, a network of fences surrounds six massive buildings offset by a long row of warehouses. Each block is slotted with windows barely wide enough to reach through. In the trap, locked in front to back, two cloned versions of the guards in Concord emerge with mirrored poles to search the undercarriage. The practice defies logic on this end of the trip. Who on earth sneaks *into* a prison?

The guard guides me down the two-stair drop from the back of the van and leads me into a plain white building on the prison's perimeter. I am handed off to an awaiting guard. Pleasantries are exchanged: "How's Concord treating you?" the Shirley guard asks. "Like a baby treats a diaper," Concord replies.

After a thorough strip search, I am led to HSU for screening. The hospital's one nurse takes my blood pressure, asks some particulars like am I allergic or HIV positive, or do I hear the voices of the dead? "Only hers," I respond. She isn't amused.

She pulls out a needle, my third tuberculosis test in a year. The prick stings, and a weal forms then subsides. Seventy-two hours of quarantine in A1 until they know I'm clear. I just want to get to a phone. Mom is probably home from visiting Kev.

They don't escort me to the block. Instead, an electric zap unlocks the door and a voice from behind the glass tells me to proceed to A1. A camera shrouded by heavy metal and a thick glass shield points down. I press the buzzer and wait. Wind slashes my face. I wait. Ring again. And wait.

I hop for warmth. I press call again. An electric surge clicks the door lock open. I enter the foyer and wait. The guard waves me in and points out the pile of folded bedding that preceded me. The block is two tiered. A podium sits center stage where the guard controls the cell doors, phones, and PA system from an elevated position.

My eyes are riveted on the phones bolted to the steel poles supporting the stairs. Against my better judgment, I ask, "Do you mind if I call home and let them know where I am?"

"No phone calls your first three days. Lock in," he says while flipping a switch that activates a door on the top tier.

My cell mate is young, twenty-something, baby faced and balding with shaggy facial hair. He gives me less than a minute to settle before asking if I want to play cards. I want to lie down and stare at the ceiling, to send Mom psychic vibes that I'm okay and will call as soon as I can. But something about the guy who

introduces himself as Carlo makes it hard for me to deny him
momentary respite from the tedium.

We play gin. He deals from the bottom and is obnoxious
when he wins. He points and snickers, comments on my skills, or
the lack thereof, as a card player. He is sluggish and telegraphs his
moves, gives them away with a flicker of his eyes, the rapidity of
his blink. I know before he does when he'll reach for his cup, and I
can tell by the way he sits that his knee is gimp. There is
something despicable about him, but he doesn't wear it like Nutsy.
He harbors his despicable nature like a parasite.

"So what'd you do?" I ask, just about fed up with him
before the first day has ended.

"I got hosed, dude," he replies, shaking his head.

"You ever met anyone in here that didn't think that?" I
throw it to gauge if Carlo is self actualized.

His face contorts. He is thrown off his tangent. "No dude,
they gave me twelve years." He doesn't give away his crime, the
magnitude of the number is supposed to precipitate the outrage he
expects me to feel.

"For what?" I ask, looking as if I already can't believe his
persecution.

"I stole a car, dude." He delivers the news after the wind
up, pitching the words as if there's to be no further inquiry.

"You got twelve years for stealing a car?" I ask, curious
because I know the crime carries a minimum of seven.

"Twelve years."

"How'd they catch you?" I ask.

Carlo gets somber, hunkers for the telling of a long tale as if he deems me a surrogate jury, one that might not convict him. "I was jacking it from a drugstore parking lot. It was dark, no one around. Just as I got the fucking door open, I see this security guard at the far end of the lot. I panicked. He called the cops because, as soon as I pulled out, a cruiser was on me." He wrings his hands as if trying to get dirt off only he can see. "I flew through a couple of lights, mostly yellows, but the last one was red. I barreled through and slammed into a dude on a bike."

"A pedal bike or a motorcycle?" I ask.

"A motorcycle."

"How bad?"

Carlo looks at me as if I asked to see suppressed evidence. "The guy got messed up, I know, but twelve years? Come on, I won't get out until I'm thirty three."

It's the first time I feel compassion for him. He's stuck in a void, using chronological age as a means of calculation. I prefer days or maybe months and stay away from adding them up into years.

"You'll still be pretty young when you get out. But I can imagine how far away that must seem to you."

"Easy for you to say. You got scrape time." He snickers and looks away.

I shrug it off. "Yeah, I guess."

"You want to see the court papers, read for yourself how I got screwed?" he asks.

I'd just as soon go through another strip search and TB test than read some lengthy court document, but I see it as a means of shutting him up for a few and so I take him up on his offer.

He fishes through his locker and produces a manila envelope busting at the seams. He pulls out the contents gingerly, as if haste will change the inflection of the testimony. He cradles what he intends me to read and seals the rest. Everybody on the inside knows that paperwork is sacred. It tells your story from a perspective few ever see, as if someone had a window seat into the blackest part of your soul and wrote down every gory detail they saw.

His victim might have been better off dead. He'll never see out of one eye, and the other never stops watering. He can barely walk, needed assistance to even take the stand, and he has tens of thousands of dollars in medical bills and can't work. Carlo's lawyer refused to cross examine, the trial's only shred of integrity. Carlo was offered ten in a plea bargain and refused it. He decided to roll the dice and take this mess of a defense, this absence of a defense, to trial.

I finish as much as I can, as much as I need to. I wish I hadn't read a letter of it. If anything, the news in these documents fuel a burgeoning gratitude for the mass of razor wire and motion detectors that keep me confined, because they also confine him and others like him, morons who have no clue what the cost of their acts might be and don't care.

Carlo sits, anxiously waiting for me to finish. His knee bounces. He squirms in his seat. I close the folder and sit up. "So? What do you think? Seriously. Did I deserve to get twelve years for that?"

I look out the window and try to focus on the woods so rudely interrupted, mowed down to make way for this affront to nature.

"You deserve every minute of your sentence, and I deserve every minute of mine."

Mother

A guard strip searches me before the visit I wasn't expecting. I notice Mom sits alone, no Grandma.

"Hi, sweetie." Mom rises and envelops me, holding on tighter than usual.

"Hey, Mum." I try to pull away but she holds me there a moment longer.

"How is it here? Any different?"

"Never mind that, what did the doctor say?" I ask.

Her face softens. "It's cancer."

"What kind?" I am afraid what it might mean to show vulnerability, but I need to know.

"Lung," she says. Tears well up in her eyes, and I fetch her some napkins.

"Can they operate?"

She nods in the negative. "No, they say it's too risky. It's stage four and spread to my stomach." She falls forward, and I catch her. "I don't want to die. I'm not ready to leave you kids," she whispers. I'm breaking the rules with contact beyond the allowed greeting and goodbye. No exceptions, the rules say.

I feel the tap on my shoulder and wish cancer upon the hand that interrupts. It's a clean shaven clone. He doesn't say a word, just gestures for me to sit back.

"What does the doctor want to do?" I ask.

"He wants to enroll me in a study. They're going to try an aggressive dose of both chemo and radiation." Her face contorts.

"Who else knows?"

"Just you. I can't tell your brother. He won't understand. He'll fly off the handle. He's so fragile that I can't tell him anything. I worry about him so." Her tears now fall freely.

"It'll be okay. He'll be okay. Don't worry about that now. Just get the treatment and fight it — we'll make it through this," I lie.

"Maybe I can call your lawyer. He might be able to petition to get you out early, given the circumstances." Hope glimmers in her eye.

"Maybe. Give him a call and see what he can do."

The same clone taps me again. "Time's up," he says. "A-1, orientation block, only gets one hour. Let's go."

Mom places a hand on my knee. "It's okay, sweetie. It's good for me to get out of here before the sun goes down. You know how bad I am in the dark."

We hug again, and she clutches to me. After the strip search, I walk slowly, in no hurry to sit in a cell with Carlo while he broods over his sentence. When I get there, I stretch out on my bunk and prop my pillow into a ball so I can look through the temepered glass, beyond fence and razor, past guard towers, at the horizon.

When she visits again, she sits in the green, thickly padded chairs daisy chained together on thick black metal frames. I slouch, forced to do so by my seat's razor-straight back that makes my muscles ache and my butt numb.

She looks horrible. I avoid staring. It looks like something inside her is hording more than its fair share of her energy, of her life. She keeps a kerchief wadded in her hand. Nausea is a way of life for her now. The chemo and radiation poison her, but Mom takes her damned-if-I-do, damned-if-I-don't catch-22 with a sense of humor, joking it must have been the weed because cigarettes don't kill people.

Occasionally, she gets up and stumbles to the bathroom. The guards watch her intently. I'm positive the cameras in the black bubbles are fixed on me as I sit, ready to choke the first guard who even hints that anything suspicious is going on. I am calmed by the rationale that they know the nuances of drugs and contraband being passed, and that my visit meets none of the criteria.

"We have to discuss the arrangements," she blurts out during a lull in conversation.

I prefer oblivion. "What arrangements?"

She shoots her never-misunderstood you-know-damn-well-what arrangements look. And with that, as she has every week she feels well enough to visit, she dispenses wisdom like she has a flip-top head and each nugget of experience pops out like Pez into my waiting cupped hands.

"I made you executer of the will," she says.

"Me?" I ask.

"Your brother needs you, and he'll always need you. He's so helpless." A tear avalanches down her sunken cheek. "I'm sorry," she says after a moment of silence while she marshals what is left of her composure. "I'm so scared. I don't want to leave you kids," she whimpers, and her neck telescopes into her chest.

A guard taps me on the shoulder because we've violated the contact rule. It's the guard that works nights on my block. She hands me a wad of folded tissues. Mom sits back and the guard walks away.

"I'm sorry."

"Don't be," I say.

"I know this is a lot to load on you, but I need you to know what I want done after I'm gone."

"You're not going anywhere, Mum, so stop it." I say the words but don't believe them.

She puts her hand on my knee. "I pray to the Goddess that you're right. But let's be realistic: you're probably not." Tears roll freely, mine and hers. "I'll watch over you, I swear. If I'm not looking up instead of down, that is."

"Yeah, well, hell has all the interesting people anyway — you'll fit right in." I laugh with her.

"I'll be waiting to jab that son-of-a-bitchin' father of yours with a red hot pitchfork. I'm serious. I'll wait an eternity to exact my revenge for him doing this to you boys." And I know she means every syllable. I tell her it's not good to die with unresolved conflicts looming, but she tells me to jam the Freud right up my ass.

Two weeks ago, the class board voted unanimously to send me to a minimum. I asked to be sent to the one closest to Mom, and instead they class me to the one furthest from her. I know it's time to go when my door cracks after morning count. The lack of bodies scurrying to get to chow tips me off. I halt mid-stride. The block is eerily quiet except for the crackling of the radio announcing that all inmates are present and accounted for. I approach the guard. He hands me a pass to property. "Pack it up. Pondville," he says.

I appreciate that the move is relaxed. No shackles. Only cuffs. Pondville has no walls, no locking doors, no motion detectors or guard towers. The place does not need them. The five years added to your sentence should the thought of escaping creep into consciousness looms like a storm cloud over the prison.

I am assigned to the highway crew. A yellow van picks us up every morning at eight and drives us to a Department of Public Works station where we gather our tools: spiked wooden poles to stick trash and yellow trash bags to fill and leave by the roadside when they won't hold another gum wrapper or beer bottle.

The van follows us as we walk. We start off in a tight formation but fan out as the day wears on. Some inmates move far enough ahead so that the guard can't see them pick up half smoked cigarette butts that they'll hide up in their rectum and smuggle into the prison. Occasionally, we come across boxes of porn, dildos, half packs of smokes, the occasional roach from a joint, half-full bottles of booze; but more often there are full diapers from someone's baby and piss bombs from truckers.

On Mondays we travel down to Foxboro to walk Route 1 after Patriots' home games and clean up the remnants of whole barbeques: rancid meat, half cases of beer, panties, and an occasional bag of weed. Since they randomly subject us to breathalyzers, most of us don't partake in anything we find. The job is monotonous, but it gets me outside.

Finally, my last week grinds down to my last night, and sleep is out of the question under the weight of the stress of all there is to do. The state sends a letter stating I have twenty-four hours to check in with probation upon release. It also says that, for the next three years, they'll keep tabs on me.

The day I step out of prison isn't at all what I imagined. I pictured more frolicking on my part, more explicit joy expressed as dancing or something. Mom's frailty shocks me. Chemo and radiation have stripped her of her pudginess, and her face is sunken and colorless. Despite an expired license, I drive so Mom can rest. She nods out, her head bobbling back and forth from the pain meds. Eventually, she lies back and sleeps.

We head straight to probation where I'm finger printed, photographed, and spoken to like I'm second-rate garbage. Alba, my probation officer, instructs me to have a seat. Her desk is chaos, all paperwork. No pictures, nothing that even hints at a life beyond the office. She regurgitates a list of rules memorized through repetition: "You'll report to me twice a month with proof of address. It has to be recent mail, no check stubs, bank statements, or personal letters." She leafs through my file with a raised eyebrow. "Do you still talk to your father?"

"Yes."

I expected a line of questions, but she closes the file dismissively. "Your probation fee is to be paid each month — no personal checks or cash."

"Then how do I pay it?" I ask.

Her eyes roll under shadow-laden lids. "Money orders or bank checks. You'll work, fulltime, and bring proof of employment every visit."

"I plan on going back to school fulltime. Does that count?"

"That's not a job. You'll work and bring proof every visit," she repeats.

Prison taught me to pick my battles wisely, and so I leave it at that.

Mom struggles to stay awake in the hospital waiting room. After a short wait, we're ushered into an examination room. The doctor breezes in, looking like he pulled his clothes from the hamper in a rush. Bags dangle under his eyes. He holds Mom's chart close to his chest.

He approaches her after shaking my hand. I step into the corner. "How do you feel?" he asks while poking and prodding her.

Mom shrugs. "Depends on what you have to tell me, really." Before he can reply, he hits a spot that makes Mom cringe in pain. He lifts her shirt to reveal a series of bruises. "I fell," she says in response to his raised eyebrows.

"When, where?" I ask, stepping closer. The bruises are ripe red and purple bursts.

"I was walking down the stairs and slipped," she replies with her chin to her chest.

The doctor sits on a rolling stool and opens the file containing her chart, a file thick with paperwork that I assume are test results and statistics about her condition.

"I received the results of your last treatments and am sorry to report that there was no change in the size of the tumors in your lungs."

I look at Mom. Her eyes mist like a rolling fog. A tear rolls down her creviced face; another clears her lower lash and plummets to the floor. "Can we try the chemo again?" she asks.

"The last round nearly did you in, and I fear another dose might kill you," he responds, flipping though pages in her chart.

"But there's a chance it might not, right?" she pleads.

"I think the best thing we can do now is try to make you as comfortable as possible. I'm sorry."

"How did she get this?" I ask. I need to hear it was her decades of smoking so he can chastise her because I can't bring myself to say it. I am angry, however. I want it said.

"It's impossible to tell," he says to me. Then to her, he says, "The important thing right now is to manage your pain and get you set up with hospice. I'm concerned about this fall. We might need to admit you if they get any worse." He ignores me altogether, probably because he can feel me glaring at him, itching to grill him. What do you mean, I want to say, that it's impossible to tell? How about an educated guess, genius: she smoked since she was twelve. Shit, I secondhand smoked two packs a day for Christ's sake. Got any theories on that, Doc? I wanted him to formulate a treatment plan for my pain. Where was the hospice for victims of the victims?

My indignation nearly bowls me over, and I pull back from that brink. This isn't about me, I remind myself. Mom's dying, the final decree spoken and scribbled in her chart. I put my arm around her while she sobs.

"I don't want to be admitted. I want to be home when it happens."

"Mum, it might be a good idea; at least they can keep an eye on you just in case anything happens."

"No, please. I don't want to… I want to be home… Please." Her face is soaked with tears. The doctor stands and removes a prescription pad from his coat pocket. I hope at least one of the five scripts he writes is for me.

"These are for more pain medication: morphine, klonopin, and something for the nausea." He hands her the scripts. She waves them off to me.

We walk arm and arm to the car, and she clutches me like a life preserver. I set her down in the passenger seat and buckle her in. She stops me before I put the keys in the ignition. "Do you remember our pact, the one we made after you were arrested?"

"Of course."

"You better," she says.

Hospice nurses and home health aides are saints who rank in the upper echelons of heaven that include those who give kidneys to strangers and eyes to the blind. Mom's mind slips from malnourishment and heavy medication. Kev calls nightly for an update, which I deliver like a news anchor, all facts and no emotion, protecting us both. Dad calls to sympathize with my plight but is unaware of my growing resentment toward him. I fault him for the time I've missed, for the days I just barely missed because I had yet to be released, days when Mom was clearer, healthier, those precious moments cancer allows you that other forms of death, say a car accident, steals.

I nap in between episodes of Mom trying to escape from the hospital she thinks she's in, trying to escape from John, the orderly she thinks I am. When she's not shunning John the orderly, she sees me and asks, "Are you disappointed?"

"In what?" I ask.

"Me as a mother?"

"Of course not. Don't be silly."

"Am I being silly? I wish I was better to you and Kevin."

"You were a great mother," I say.

"Liar. I was drunk half the time. How can you say that?"

"You had your issues. But that's in the past now. Come on, now. Stop this."

"No, there's no time left. I want you to promise me you'll take care of your brother. He's so angry. Promise you'll help him."

"I promise," rolls out automatically, like the subsequent shriek following the jab of a red hot poker. I am branded with a deathbed pledge.

John the Orderly

Stillness permeates the room, the world. Life halts in death's presence. The bird feeder perches are bare. The ducks huddle quietly in their house. Storm clouds hold the light hostage: 18 hours left, hospice says. Time to rally the troops.

I phone, in order of seniority, Grandma, Mom's sisters, and finally Kev. He's harder to reach because prisons don't take messages. When he calls, I update him.

"Hospice says she only has a few hours left," I say. He remains silent, holding together. "She can't talk. She just lays there and shakes." I wait. Nothing. "Do you want to say goodbye to her?"

"Yeah," he says.

I put the phone to her ear. She shakes and convulses, mouthing, "No."

I pull the phone away. "I have to go." Kev says, and he hangs up, leaving me to worry about how he'll process this. Kev uses drugs to cope where I have more sophisticated means. At night, after the hospice nurse leaves, I line up Mom's meds on the counter in the kitchen and read the labels: 24-hour slow release morphine, sublingual morphine, klonopin, and Percocet. But it isn't the desire to take them that soothes me as much as the ability to think the craving through to the consequences. Besides, opiates were never my thing — I liked stimulants.

Being in the same room with her is almost more than I can bear, but I remain. I sit on the edge of the bed and watch. Her jaw moves as if she presents her case to the Grim Reaper himself, who doesn't care one way or the other, of course. It's the journey he's responsible for, nothing more. Her eyes search the ceiling, possibly for more of her deceased relatives who have visited on more than one occasion. As I fed her, she'd look over my shoulder and ask, "Who's that?"

"I'm not sure," I'd reply, confident we were alone. "What do they look like?"

"See for yourself. It's my Uncle Teddy, I think, but he's different." One side of her face is bathed in lamplight, the other eclipsed by night.

"How so?" I ask, shifting, uncomfortable in my conviction that I can in fact feel the presence of ghosts.

"He's covered in light."

"What does he want?" I asked.

"He wants me to go with him," she replied.

"Maybe you should go."

"Are you kidding? He drinks."

"So did you."

She smirked then and looked at me, and I recognized her. So much of the time she was drugged and delusional, someone else, but I knew this was her, my mother, looking at me. These moments were rare, however. I'd often wake to the thud of her frail frame hitting the floor after she fell trying to make it to the closet to pack. I'd lift her and place her back in bed under protest. "Leave me alone, John! I want to be discharged! You can't keep me here!" she barked. In fact, most of my time was spent glued to the baby monitor I bought so I could hear when she tried to escape.

As John, the orderly, I could embody all the traits I lacked as Bryan: I was stronger, capable of treating her as she needed to be treated in order to get her through the day. I was calmer, more reserved in the face of her suffering, more resolute that death is indeed part of life, albeit the end for her and a terrible ordeal for me. Besides, John protected me. Helping Mom bathe and go to the bathroom was difficult as her son, but not as John.

"Time to get up to pee and brush your teeth," John ordered, wheeling the walker into place.

"I'll go but I don't want the walker," she'd say, casting disparaging looks at me and the walker, loathing it as much as John's intrusion.

"You need the walker. We've discussed this. No walker, no meds," John said, capable of stating it plainly, without the sharp edge I'd have added.

"Fine. But I'll do it myself, without your help."

"Do what you want, but if you take another nasty spill, the nurse says you'll have to be moved downstairs," John replied.

We'd shuffle to the bathroom where John helped Mom pee. At the sink, Mom turned her head toward John at his behest and smiled so he could brush her teeth.

"Okay, now back to bed. Let's go," John ordered.

Back at the bedside, Mom reached under her pillow for a lighter and pack of smokes hidden there. I chuckled; amazed that she still craved what was killing her. John the orderly hovered over her. "Haven't those things done enough damage?"

Mom smirked and shrugged. "Not like quitting is going to help me now, so fuck it."

It was good to hear her say "fuck it" again. There were so many times growing up, when money was tight, that she'd whip out the checkbook at Caldor's department store or Rich's and hit what I affectionately called the fuck-it button, that automatic override on her budgeting calculator that dispelled any thoughts of saving for a rainy day. I loved the fuck-it button.

Dad calls from prison. He must have tried to console Kevin. I listen to the recording, tempted to press nine, the magic number that permanently blocks inmates from calling. My animosity grows. I blame him for robbing me of the precious few months left with Mom.

"Hi son," he says after I accept the call.

"Hey, Dad."

"Your brother told me what's going on. I'm sorry," he says.

"Thanks."

"I wish you weren't shouldering this alone, son, but as you know, there's nothing your brother and I can do from here."

"I know."

"Well, maybe it's all for the best."

I imagine Dad's brain working something like the Terminator's, every possible response to a human interaction displayed across his field of vision. "All for the best" is just under "Maybe it'll all work out" and "Time heals all wounds."

"Maybe," I reply, keeping the conversation moving toward an end.

"How ya holding up, son?" he asks.

"Fine."

"Well, I'll give you a call tomorrow to see how you're doing. Take care, son."

"I will."

What's been building in me bubbles over after I hang up the phone. The neighborhood fills with a crack that repeats as if thirty home runs had been hit in a row. But the sound is empty of the thrill of victory, the hammering an assault on nature. Armed with a Louisville slugger deep in the woods near the house, my rage finds an outlet on an unsuspecting oak.

Death Watched

As a rule, Death is neither early nor late, nor is he on time as if there were some deadline to be met. There are factors that make his arrival a less than exact science and more an estimation. She is ready. What the cancer hasn't taken is dim and fading, but she refuses to face him, and so he waits.

Her son tiptoes in with a tray, and places it down gingerly. He sits down, and Death acquaints himself with the surroundings, trinkets collected as reminders of places visited, symbols of ideologies long held dear.

For the past sixty days, she has subsisted on room temperature Ensure and morphine. She reaches for her smokes. Her son watches her nod out while she inhales.

"Where's Kevin?" she asks.

"He's in prison, Mum."

Her face contorts. "Bryan, my Bryan. Please take care of him. He needs you."

"I know, Mum. I will," he replies.

Tears roll, hers and his. "He's so angry. He won't be able to handle this." She looks to where Death stands in the shadows. "What's he doing here?" she asks.

"Who?" Her son asks.

"That guy." She points to the corner.

"I don't know. What's he want?"

She ponders the question a moment. "He's here to get me."

"So go," he says.

"Fuck that."

"Well, you didn't go when Uncle Teddy came."

"Well, this guy's creepier than Uncle Teddy."

"Mum, lie down. I need to change your bandage."

She acquiesces. Her son exposes the bandage that covers her stomach, peeling it back. Death shifts from one shadow to another, moving steadily closer. The tumor threatens to breach her abdomen. Death watches her son's reaction to his stench. Not long now.

When her son leaves, she stares at Death, who stares back. "I can't go yet. I don't want to leave my kids."

No answer.

"Fuck you!" She screams.

By nightfall, she falls into a trance. Death puts her where no one can reach her. Her eyes fall blank. She shivers. Her eyes fail to close or blink. Death marks her passing by extinguishing the candles, one by one. While the last one flickers, he pulls her from her vessel.

Mom draws her last breath just after midnight, her mother, one of her sisters, and friends from work present. I get up from my place at Mom's side to leave but stop in the doorway. My grandmother stands and walks to my mother's side. "Lucy?" she sobs. "Lucy? Lucille? No, no, please, Lucy."

My aunt leads Grandma away while I call the town's only funeral home. "We'll send someone right over," they say.

A minivan pulls into the driveway. Two men unload a stretcher with a body bag laid out on top. I show them to Mom but think better of watching them work. When they are done, they ask, "What do you want to show her in?"

"Show her in?" I reply, feeling my aunt behind me, closing in to explain. She accompanies me to Mom's closet to pick out an outfit.

By the time everyone leaves, it's three in the morning. The house settles into an eerie silence. Darkness envelops the place. I can only seem to recall what the hospice nurse told me that day: "People report strange things happening in the days following someone's passing."

"Like?" I had asked.

"One woman reported the toilet seat up every time she went to the bathroom, something she constantly bickered about with her husband. Others wake to the sound of doors closing or pots and pans rattling."

"And you think that'll happen here?" I asked.

"No. I'm just saying not to be too freaked out if it does."

"Well, thank you for everything. You, all of the people at hospice, really made this more bearable. Really, thanks so much." I start getting emotional and so she puts her hand on my shoulder and simply says, "Our pleasure," before leaving.

The wake is something Mom and I discussed — and something she never wanted. "I hate the idea of everyone standing around sobbing. I'd rather people just go to the church service," she said while I squirmed in my seat.

Mom planned her own service, music and all. She chose the songs to be played by a guitarist and vocalist she knew. The service was held in a small Unitarian Church near the house, a place she knew my Polish grandmother would resent.

"What kind of church is that?" Babchi asks when I tell her where the service is to be held.

"It's a Unitarian church, one that accepts all faiths," I reply.

"But she's Catholic. She doesn't need anything but a Catholic church," Babchi says in a tone reminiscent of my childhood, when she ruled the family with an iron fist, one she was unafraid to hammer you with.

"Babchi, Mom was Wiccan, not Catholic; she wanted to tell you but was afraid of how you'd react. She took the time to plan her own service at a church she felt accepted in and loved."

Part frustration at Mom for keeping her religion a secret, part insolence at Babchi's fascist rule, I speak the truth, intending to cause whiplash.

"I won't go," Babchi says.

"Fine, if that's how you feel. I guess Mom was right about not telling you."

At this she softens, her shoulders, slumped since Mom died, fall further into surrender. "So, what? There will be firecrackers and hula-hoops?" she says softly, then looks up at me and smiles.

"Not quite, but close," I reply, laughing.

I opt for one showing in a rented casket, since Mom's wish is to be cremated. Babchi, clad all in black, flanks me as I take my place next to Mom. Family members walk in, pay their respects, and offer words of consolation before moving off to join those scattered throughout the showroom. Mom is made up in the outfit we chose. Her eyes are shut, arms folded neatly across her midsection. I remember what Mom said about being waked: "Lay me face down so I can see where I'm going, and so everyone can kiss my white ass goodbye."

When the service is over, I sit with Mom a few extra minutes before they wheel her off to be cremated. They say I can pick up the ashes in a week. Her wish is for Kev and me to spread them anywhere in the White Mountains, where she loved to camp. At home I step into her room and sit at the end of the bed she spent close to three month in. Against my better judgment, I keep a few bottles of the leftover meds. Some might call it a plan to relapse, but I found them fitting souvenirs. Keeping the bottles reminds me of how easy it would be to return to ignorant bliss, where for a short time, I won't feel a thing.

Because of the mere suggestion of paranormal activity by the hospice nurse, I turn the clock radio on, mute the TV, and bathe in flickers. I haven't been this paranoid since I smoked my last half ounce of coke. If I find something out of place, my heart sinks and it keeps me awake.

As a kid, I had trouble sleeping if the closet door was open. Mom hated whenever I fell asleep with my radio on. So she'd come up and shut it off. I left it on to summon her, to distract her, if even for a few seconds, from her bottle. Before she left, she'd tuck me in and kiss me softly on the cheek.

I begin to doze as Channel 4 hands the network over to paid sponsors. Between nods, I notice the closet door halfway open. As the sun rises, I wake to a closed closet door, an extinguished TV, and a dead quiet radio. I try desperately to recall, or even manufacture, the memory of getting up to do all these things, anything to avoid facing my worst fear: Mom is fucking with me.

I can't take any more constant worry that I'll one day face Mom's transparent form, draped white, or worse, in red, garnished with a trident and forked tongue. As soon as it's late enough, the ducks and bunnies fed, I open the phone book to therapists. It's time I see a scientist, one who can reassure me that goblins don't exist. I choose a man who specializes in addiction. My appointment is set for three that afternoon.

The waiting room of his office does little to sooth my reticence. Instead of the warm neutral tones of my mind's eye, the walls are stark white and pinged here and there, from moving furniture, or was there a scuffle over diagnoses, I wonder? I sit and flip through *Time Magazine*.

Dr. Wainwright, who is stout, walks like a T-rex, swinging from the hips rather than a normal heel-toe step. He steps up and shakes my hand with an iron grip that I shake loose when he turns to lead me into his office. A large desk is against the wall. Two high-backed chairs face off. A marker board is nailed high on the wall. He sits down on the chair farthest from the door and crosses his tree trunk legs.

The overhead florescent light is off, and two lamps temper the room in a soft glow. "So, what brings you in today?" he asks.

I vaguely remember sitting, and when exactly I grabbed the chair's only pillow and clutched it like a teddy bear I can't recall at all. I notice that he notices, so I discard the pillow on the floor. "My Mom passed away last week." I adopted "passed away" after spewing "she's dead" at one of her creditors calling about a past due invoice. I had clearly intended to stun the caller, but instead I found myself reeling under the weight of those words.

"Oh, I'm sorry. How did she die?" he asks.

"Adenocarcinoma of the lung, or so said the official death certificate."

"I see. Smoker?" he asks.

"Two packs a day," I reply.

"Around you?"

"Oh, I secondhand smoked at least a pack a day."

"That must have been tough for you."

"Not as bad as her drinking."

"She was an alcoholic?"

"The best."

"Your Dad too?"

"Nah, Dad doesn't do anything."

"I see. And you? Do you drink?" he asks.

"No. I used to, but now I'm in recovery. So was she when she died, in recovery for ten years."

"How long for you?"

"Four years."

"Do you go to meetings?"

"No."

"Why not?"

"Because I can't find peace in those fucking things," I say, aware of how defensive I sound.

He remains quiet and nods, obviously backing off. Perhaps he sits back farther in his chair or maybe I perceive him as smaller, but either way, it is my anger that fills the room.

"I did go initially, and it did help. It gave me structure, a place to go instead of hanging with old friends, but after a while I felt I needed something more, more of an explanation as to why

I'm an addict. I needed answers to questions the twelve steps couldn't provide."

"What about the support it provides?" he asks. I feel like he's leading me somewhere I don't want to go.

"The support?"

"Yes, the fellowship."

I guess that he's in recovery, or at least has spent significant time at meetings because he uses the word fellowship, a word in the AA preamble the attendees recite before every meeting. "I don't know. I guess I never thought about it that way."

"Maybe you should."

"Maybe."

I leave thinking about what he said. I know there's a meeting not far from the house tonight. At home, the house is once again eerily quiet. I don't enter any room without turning on a light first. By the end of the night, every night, all the lights in the house blare — until I get the first electric bill. Mom's death forces me to be more responsible, more organized. I keep track of all of Mom's affairs with a checking account, something I never needed while I was using drugs because I never paid bills. Bills were just suggestions to pay. The consequences meant nothing, and when the shit hit the fan, I called Dad and he sent a check.

I go to the meeting and see the same people still struggling to stay clean who were here when I attended last. I go to get out of the house and to take my therapist's suggestion seriously. I know I won't find fellowship here, though. There's something underlying that blocks my acceptance of the twelve steps. I scan them, hung prominently in the front of the room. God is in six of them, and yet everyone scoffs at this point and says, "It's not religious; it's spiritual." To me, that's like saying, "They're feelings, not emotions."

Afterwards, I head home. Fall is peppering the leaves with color. The ducks try in vain to protect their eggs from the fox that lives in the woods nearby. One night, before Mom got sick, I woke to her banging the window and shining a flashlight down on the pond next to the house where the ducks nested during the summer. "Goddamn it! Get away from those ducks!" she screamed loud enough to wake neighbors.

"Mom, what the fuck are you yelling at?" I shouted.

"That goddamn fox is stealing eggs from Emma!" she screeches. "Go down there and scare it!"

I didn't argue. I knew that it was best to do as I was told. Walking down the stairs, clueless as to what scared hungry foxes, I grabbed a copy of the past-due property tax bill that scared the hell out of Mom. I also grabbed a pot and wooden spoon. In my boxer briefs, I ran toward the pond, clanging the pot and yelling in chorus with Mom in the window, providing the only light.

The next day I came home to an unmarked van parked in the driveway. Inside I found Mom and a man I'd never met before, a professional trapper. "Normally I'd set a few traps and catch the thing, but with kids in the neighborhood, I can't," he said. "What I can do is give you these," and he handed Mom what looked like M-80s.

"These are quarter sticks," he continued, "and they are illegal without a permit, so you never got them from me. All you do is find the hole and chuck one in."

Mom nodded. I was sure she'd throw the dynamite away and never give it a second thought. She paid the man for his time and for the quarter sticks. I waited patiently for us to laugh and make fun of him. Instead, Mom handed me the sticks without instructions since I already heard what to do.

"You can't be serious," I said.

"I want you to find that hole and blow that thing straight to hell." Her eyes flared.

"Mom, these are quarter sticks of dynamite. You know, T-N-T."

She raised an eyebrow, and I knew to back off because Mom couldn't voluntarily raise an eyebrow; it was an involuntary response, a warning not to continue debating. "Do you know where the term 'sitting duck' comes from?" She didn't wait for a response. "It's because ducks on a nest never leave their eggs. They'll die before they leave them, and I'll be damned if I'm going stand idly by while Emma gets devoured by that goddamn fox."

She forced the sticks into my hand. I turned to go but she stopped me. "Wait, you'll need this." She handed me a lighter.

I found the fox hole halfway between the house and the city dump. If I returned and feigned success, she'd ask, in a voice I would only hear as Marvin the Martian's, "Where's the earth-shattering ka-boom? There was supposed to be an earth-shattering ka-boom."

The earth-shattering ka-boom shook the forest floor, and no doubt, drew the attention of the fox safe in his hole. I possessed the intestinal fortitude to point a loaded gun at someone's face, but lacked the callousness to toss a bomb into a fox's hole. His only crime was to answer the call of his growling stomach, and who was I to interrupt nature's design?

"You couldn't do it, could you?" Mom asked, swinging in the lawn chair when I returned.

"Nope," I replied.

She smiled. "Good."

Dr. Wainwright looks me over, probably wondering if I'm clean. "I'm so tired. I can't sleep in that house," I say.

"Is there somewhere else you can go?" he asks.

"My grandmother's."

"Is that an option?"

"Yes and no. She's old, and I know she'll just fuss over me relentlessly."

"Is that a bad thing?" he asks.

"It depends. She's the kind of person that'll do my laundry day in and day out with no complaints. Mind you, I won't ask her to. She'll just do it. Then one day she'll freak out and start screaming about it until I say forget it, until I say I'll do it from now on. But she won't let me do the laundry — she'll just want to yell about it."

"Sounds very passive aggressive," he says.

"Totally. Plus she's a fierce racist," I add.

"How so?"

"I remember one Thanksgiving. Kev and I were driving her home from a restaurant. We started having Thanksgiving at restaurants because she was an awful cook. Anyway, we drove by some projects where some kids were playing in a baseball field. Out of nowhere she blurts out, 'It's a good goddamn thing we keep those niggers behind fences.' We were mortified, hearing our eighty year-old grandmother say something like that."

"She grew up in the depression, then?" Dr. Wainwright asks.

"Yeah, she'd cross a desert to save a nickel on sand."

"So she is frugal?"

"Frugal is an understatement. Once I threw out some wheat bran that I didn't want and found it the next day in the cupboard. She took it out of the trash and ate it."

"I see. Have you thought about what we discussed last time?" he asked.

"What? AA? Yeah, I went. Honestly, I hate it. I leave so angry. I can't imagine that's good for me."

"Why do you leave angry?"

"I'm not sure. I mean, I used to love going. Maybe it's because no one in there ever seems to get better. Since I left over four years ago, the same people are there complaining about the same things. Plus, I hate the fact that a religion is so adamant about not being a religion." I say.

"I agree with you on most of that. Do you think you might be able to leave that aside and focus on the fellowship? I really think, if you can do that, you'd benefit."

"How?" I ask.

"It'll give you a sense of community, a place to feel accepted. It strikes me that you never talk about friends. Do you have many?" Dr. Wainwright folds his hands over his stomach, mirroring my relaxed state. I intend to remain resolute that AA won't help me, but the good doctor is relentless.

"I have plenty," I lie.

"Well, adult children of alcoholics usually have a difficult time cultivating meaningful relationships. Do you think that's true of you?"

I nod yes. "What about being an adult child makes it so hard?" I ask.

He stands and pops open a marker from the tray under a marker board fixed to the wall. "Normal people experience emotions on a scale." He draws what looks like soft waves lapping a beach. "Adult children tend to be numb, and who can blame you. Sometimes adult children of alcoholics use to feel. If you want to feel sad, you use depressants, and to feel elated, stimulants." He draws what an EKG of my emotions might look like, extreme peaks and low valleys. "Adult children volley between numb and extremes, dizzying heights of elation followed by crushing depression, but otherwise, they're numb."

"So I'm numb?"

"Aren't you?"

I don't feel anything but anger. The session ends. It is our last.

Hallucinations

I don't believe in ghosts, goblins, fairies, hobbits, boogey men or women, werewolves, Nosferatu, or anything other than purely scientific reasons for things that go bump in the night. I'm not sure about God only because of my fear of judgment day. My plan to escape eternal damnation is pleading complete and total ignorance.

The TV is on. I drift. Wake. Drift. Wake. I sit up; finish a cup of instant coffee, my fourth since nightfall. My back aches, so I turn on my side, my favorite position. I drift to the clock's digits: 3:17 a.m.

My eyes peel back, digits blare: 3:20. I'm paralyzed. I can't even blink. The room is bright. I see her feet peripherally, nothing else. I can't move. My eyes grow dry. The desire to blink, to shake loose this hallucination, to wake up with a start, sweat-drenched, panicked and confused, is a blessing denied, because I'm stone cold conscious. I make out what looks like a black dress. No, not a dress. A gown, a graduation gown. I can't look, can't turn my head to face her. She calls out my name once and is gone, and with her, my last hope of a decent night's sleep.

The next day, Marcel, my college professor, invites me to dinner. He picks me up to take me to a restaurant not far from the house. We exchange pleasantries. Marcel reminisces during dinner. "Do you remember what you used to do during my lectures?"

"Yup, I listened intently and took detailed notes."

His hee-haw laugh attracts attention from other tables. "Hardly. You'd come in, march to the back row, and place your closed notebook and capped pen on top of your desk."

"You saw that?"

He grins. The waitress brings us cake.

"So I hear you used to be a priest before becoming a professor," I say.

"Well, no. I was a pastor."

"Quite the transition."

"I'll say." He looks out the window. Ducks wade through the pond in back of the restaurant. "I believe in God. I was ready to devote my life to the church. But the more I looked, the less I found God in church doctrine and the more I found him everywhere else, and so I left the church and went back to school."

"For a Masters?"

"Actually, two: one in theology and one in psychology, and I took a doctorate in psychotherapy." He rattles this off as if taking inventory of his body: two eyes, a nose, three advanced degrees.

"Wow, that's impressive," I say.

"I guess. I'll tell you though; I'd trade it for the kind of experience you bring to a unit."

"Me?" I ask, thrown off guard.

"I've never had a problem with substances, nor have I traveled through hell like you. I'd trade degrees for that experience any day. It makes you a great counselor."

"Thanks."

"Want to talk about why you're not sleeping?" he asks, peering at me over his glasses.

"How'd you... Is it that obvious?"

"I think only a raccoon would misinterpret those circles under your eyes." He slides his glasses up his prominent nose.

"I'm fine."

"Uh-huh."

It's my turn to stare at the ducks. "I saw her," I say after a drawn out pause.

"Go on."

"She sat on the bed and called my name. Then she was gone," I admit as plainly as possible.

"And you understand this how?" he asks, forking a piece of cake but not eating it, averting his eyes, allowing a private confession.

"I don't."

"What do you believe happened?"

"Nothing. I dreamt it."

He looks out the window again. "I believe our bodies are merely vessels carrying us through life. When our vessels are unable to carry us through any longer, we shed them and occupy a vessel that will carry us through the next phase. Maybe she was just letting you know she crossed over."

Nothing more is said. Marcel insists on paying. We drive home in silence as he digests his meal and I digest his philosophy. I sleep, undisturbed, through the night.

The phone wakes me from a sound sleep. "Hi son," Dad says after I accept the charges.

"Hey," I reply.

"I was wondering if you might be able to find out what I need to do to get my retirement fund out of Scientific Devices and into Fidelity."

Dad sold computer test equipment for Scientific Devices, traveling an expanse of five states for the better part of nineteen years. He was the first member of his family to attend college and graduated from Wentworth School of Technology with honors.

"Your retirement fund?" I ask, masking my offence.

"I'm sure I'll have to grant you power of attorney, but that's not an issue. Then all you have to do is contact Fidelity and have them transfer the money. Do you think you can do that for me, son?"

So far, not a word about the last few days of hell I have gone through. No condolences. No sympathy. He still has *his* mother, I tell myself. "Sure, Dad. As soon as I clean up the huge mess here with Mom's creditors and finish settling her estate, I'll work on yours," I say, but the sarcasm escapes him.

"Thanks, son. I heard about Mom. Boy, it must have been rough for you, but you sound okay, a little tired though. Listen, they're calling us to count. I'll call you in a few days to get an update. Bye, son." The phone line falls dead. I savor the silence pouring through the receiver before slamming it down repeatedly, slamming it until my knuckles bleed. Then I stomp on it a few times while profanity rolls off my tongue like hardcore rap. I'm aware of the pain meds I kept and the fact that relapses begin with a plan, like suicide. Rarely an impulse, behaviors invariably surface beforehand.

Winter's breath precedes its embodiment. Nights chill the landscape. The ducks huddle for warmth while I bathe in firelight. The pill bottles are perched on the hearth. Weakness prevents me from reducing them to cinders. I'm never really sure how close I am to relapse until it dawns on me that I place clarity above numbness. From atop a fresh log about to be enveloped by flame, the pill bottles sear, the labels catch and melt into a crackling firestorm of pharmaceutical fireworks, cracking and hissing in protest at my decision to stay clean.

With relapse averted, I turn my attention to dating. If instant gratification can't come from substances, then I'll find it in women. A number flashes on the screen promising to connect me with hot, single women in my area aching to chat. I'm connected to a recording of a sultry voice that thanks me for calling and tries to seduce me into entering a valid credit card number. I'm on a touch tone phone but it's an older version, one that clicks commensurate with the number pressed. This angers the recording, which interrupts my button pushing with a stern apology and asks me to hold while she connects me to a real operator. I panic and hang up.

My addiction lent itself to isolation, partly because of the stigma and partly because I didn't want to share. When I was high, I dialed 900 numbers out of loneliness, just to talk. At Plymouth State, I once racked up a $3000 phone bill calling 900 numbers during a coke binge. That was prior to the robberies, just after Dad was ripped off by our first victim and money was tight, and so Dad was furious. My denials fell on deaf ears because charges for calls to 900 numbers appeared on his phone bill every so often. In a stern voice, he just said, "Fix it," before hanging up on me. When I ordered the service I opted for a 900 number block, much the same way Dr. Jekyll opts to protect the innocent from Mr. Hyde by locking himself away. The phone company then cancelled the charges and Dad shut off the phone.

I call an ex-girlfriend, Shelly, a woman I met in AA. At the time, she was newly sober and I had a few short months under my belt. Our relationship crashed and burned after she relapsed and I heeded my sponsor's warning that coexistence with an active addict is risky. I don't ask if she's clean when she answers the phone. She's the only human contact I've had in days. She agrees to come over.

The prospect is intimidating. Prior to prison, I hadn't had too many serious relationships, just flings. Shelly arrives. She's curvier than I remember. We sit by the fire and chat.

"Sorry about your mom," she says, tilting her head. Auburn strands follow the curvature of her cheeks. She sips a glass of water I set out for us.

"Thanks," I reply.

We watch a movie and cuddle. Halfway through, I make a move and try to kiss her. She responds. Clothes are removed. We move to the floor in front of the fire. I kneel, jockeying for a better position to relieve her of her panties. Then it hits me, what can only be described as the smell low tide. Shelly's lack of hygiene makes her potent enough to make my eyes water. What was once my full-fledged readiness to perform shrinks like a frightened turtle.

I excuse myself to the bathroom and cleanse my sense of smell by inhaling the scent of hand soap. Maybe her funk is a fluke, I tell myself. Everybody experiences that not-so-fresh feeling sometimes. Maybe she's having a bad day. Either way, I have to make a decision: go back in and finish the job or bow out as gracefully as possible. As soon as I hit the threshold of the room, I know. "Sorry, Shelly. I thought I was ready for this, but I'm not."

"What is it?" she asks.

"It's just too soon. I'm still grieving."

"Aw, you poor thing. Come here." She cuddles up to me on the couch. I take shallow breaths.

Crisis number one avoided, it is time to get her out of here so I can clean up and put this unpleasantness behind me. "Would you mind if we cut this short. I'm really tired and just want to go to bed?"

"Sure thing, sweetie. Will you call me tomorrow?"

When I say, "Absolutely," I really mean, "No chance."

Alba, my probation officer, summons me to her office. "Everything taken care of in New Hampshire?" she asks, forgoing any salutations.

"Well, no. I still haven't decided if I'm going to sell the house or try to keep it. The property taxes are…" She interrupts, blurting, "Under the conditions of your probation, you are remanded back to the state. I want you gainfully employed, and fulltime."

"So, what do I do about the house?" I ask, which is less a request for advice and more a plea for leniency.

"Not my problem," she replies, peering over small, rimmed glasses.

"Of course not."

"Gainfully employed, fulltime, understood?" she asks.

"Yeah."

"Where will you live?"

"My grandmother's, probably."

"You need to bring proof of residency every time you come in," she continues, ceasing to look up from her file folder that includes a recent photo of me along with a several page description of my crimes.

"What qualifies as proof?"

"Recent mail, but not from your bank, a credit card statement, but never personal correspondence," she says. "You have your fee?"

I stand and hand her a cashier's check for forty dollars and wait. "You can go. See you in a month," she states, satisfied I've stood in awkward silence long enough.

Less than a well-constructed dwelling, more like splinters holding hands, grandma's house was built back when neighbors across the street operated a dairy farm. The once vibrant yellow aluminum siding now looks like a faded pee stain. The floor creaks under every step. A ramp from the garage brings me to the front door. Grandma's ex-husband, whom she waited on hand and foot, was crippled by type I diabetes and a host of heart issues. He died from complications arising from pneumonia.

Grandma insists she'll be fine on the pullout couch in the sun parlor so that I can have both bedrooms upstairs. "Oh, it's so nice to have you here. Now you can take me to see the boys every weekend," she says, gathering my things despite my insistence she leave them for me. "I'll do your laundry, so don't worry about that,

SUn4Q16jjC

Un4Q16jjC/-1 of 1-/premium-uk/0 A3

Thank
you for
shopping
at
Amazon.co.uk!

Packing slip for
Your order of 12 December 2024
Order ID 205-0617535-5665920

Packing slip number Un4Q16jjC
Shipping date 13 December 2024

Qty.	Order Summary	Bin
1	**Family Jewels** Paperback. Sobolewski, Mr Bryan. 061570171X : 061570171X: 9780615701714	

We hope you enjoy your gift, and we'd love to see you soon at www.amazon.co.uk

D/Un4Q16jjC/-1 of 1-//AMZL-DIG1-ND/premium-uk/0/1214-01:00/1213-08:15 Pack Type : A3 and I'll cook so you don't have to worry about that either." She storms off before I can protest. Alone in a dusty room, I slump on the bed and remember my probation officer saying, "Gainfully employed, fulltime."

I figure school will suffice for a fulltime job, and the college application I requested comes in the mail. Salem State is reputed to have a decent psychology department. I peruse the application, coming to a dead stop at question #5: *Have you ever been convicted of a felony?* I contemplate answering no but am afraid they may do a background check. Seeking guidance, I find Grandma sitting at the table sipping coffee. I act like I'm looking for something in the drawer.

"Is there something you need, darling?" she asks.

"I need a black pen for my college application."

She fishes through a drawer and pulls one from a bunch held by elastic. "There you go, sweetheart. how's it going?"

"It asks if I've ever been convicted of any felonies."

She stands as straight as her eighty year-old spine allows. "You tell them nothing!" she snaps.

I want to agree, but I play devil's advocate. "What if they check?"

She holds her hand up. "It's none of their business what you did. You tell them no, and if they ask, you lie."

I laugh, thinking she's joking. "I can't lie."

"You can and you will. It's none of their business what happens in this family. You're a good boy and so is your father. He must have been tricked, or maybe a girl tricked him." She waves me off and walks away.

I go back upstairs, answer the question in the negative, and send off the application, hoping they don't call my bluff.

Suspect

Two masked assailants wait in a stolen car; checking and rechecking to make sure their clips are full and one is in the chamber. The location is perfect: a small store at the base of a highway off ramp. An interstate one mile away will make it impossible to tell where they go.

Waiting since early morning, the target materializes. He pulls in and exits a large sedan. The robbers move with precision, pull in on his passenger side and fly out the doors. He gives up the keys while staring down the barrels of two loaded weapons. As they drive away, he draws his .357 magnum and squeezes off rounds indiscriminately. A few hit the car but none do enough damage to stop the marauders. They drive off with an entire product line in the trunk, worth more than five hundred grand.

Leaving school the next day, my heart sinks when I notice that an unmarked cruiser tails me home and pulls into the driveway behind me. Two detectives get out. "Good evening. Mind if we ask you a few questions?" asks the driver. The other scans the house and peers into my car's backseat.

"What about?" I ask.

"How about your whereabouts on Tuesday morning around nine?" he asks, brandishing a notepad and scribbling like he knows the answer.

Knowing the possibility that anything I say will be misquoted to a grand jury, I get nauseous. "Every Tuesday I have statistics from nine to eleven thirty in Brown Hall, Room 212."

"This can be verified?" the detective asks.

"Attendance is taken every class and I haven't missed any."

"And you go to Salem State, right?"

"Isn't that where you tailed me from?"

The detectives exchange glances as Grandma emerges from the house. "What's going on here?" she asks, looking more frail than normal, a shawl wrapped around her soft, ample frame.

"Nothing. Go back inside," I snap.

"Who are you?" she asks the detectives.

"I'm Detective Shaw, and this is Detective Sprankle, ma'am."

"Detectives? Why? What's going on?" she asks.

"Nothing, ma'am. I assure you this is all routine."

"Routine?" I ask.

"You see, ma'am, a jewelry store was robbed Tuesday morning and we were wondering if your grandson here had any information that might help us."

"I don't know anything about it. Now, if you'll excuse me, I need to go call my lawyer," I say, knowing that, if they had anything on me, I'd be in the back of their cruiser.

"We'll be in touch. You're on probation, right?" asks the quiet one. I grasp grandma's arm before she can turn to answer.

Inside, she says, "Sons of bitches! Who are they to come here? Sons of bitches should be grateful I don't scratch their eyes out."

I wait all night for probation to call, or worse, for the two dicks to come back and arrest me. Our phone conversations are accompanied by a click because of the court order that approved our phone being tapped. Two unmarked cars wait at either ends of the street as a reminder that ex-cons make the best suspects. I know that it's possible my encounter with the detectives never came to Alba's attention, or maybe she just hasn't gotten the word. Communication between agencies is excruciatingly slow. Either that or she knows about the detectives' visit and waits, like me, for the outcome of their investigation. Either way, she plays her cards close to the chest, revealing nothing. I offer only my usual proof of residency and a cashier's check when I see her next. She still insists I work, unsatisfied with my fulltime student status. In response, I take the personal trainer certification test offered every three months by the American Council on Exercise. With my history in fitness, I figure the test will be a cinch. When the text book arrives in the mail, I realize how much work I have ahead.

The results I get six weeks later break down each section of the test from assessments to ethical standards of personal training. I score a C on each part and don't fail any. My next step is to apply to health clubs.

I chose fitness for two reasons: One is that I've been around it for the better part of my adult life, and two, because I figured there was no way they'd do background checks.

"We've checked you out, and you're clean," says detective Shaw, standing in the driveway, intercepting me again.

"Tell me something I don't know. Mind untapping my phone now?" I ask.

"We were wondering if you might know who pulled that job?" he asks, blowing off my request.

"You ask like I know a network of scumbags that do this kind of thing — I don't. I have no idea who did it, only that is wasn't me."

"Ah, well, if you think of anything, let us know."

"Sure thing," I say, adding, "asshole," under my breath. Ex-offenders can't visit other inmates without permission from the prison's superintendent. Grandma fills out the form, insistent that I accompany her instead of just dropping her off every Sunday. It comes back marked incomplete because a letter from my probation officer is required, one that attests to my compliance with the terms of my release. Alba agrees to write it but takes her time doing so, which is fine with me. I have no desire to return to the confinement side of any wall.

I stare at a computer screen at school. Suddenly the center of my field of vision blurs, warning me that a blistering migraine is coming. Sometimes I can judge the severity based on how much sight I lose to the aura. By the time I leave, I can barely see.

The drive is one long prayer, or rather, the same short one repeated over and over: Please God, just let me get home. Red lights, distracted drivers, traffic in general are all mini-conspiracies. Once home, I mumble warnings to Grandma to stifle her obsession with home remedies. Inevitably, they only detract from the one thing that works — sleep. The left drawer of my desk contains every migraine medication known to man, including a nasal spray, which triggers cravings for something better to put up my nose, and ancient caffeine/aspirin suppositories. Apparently, my doctor thought it prudent to bypass normal digestion by inserting the cure up my ass, but I just can't seem to get past the idea of planting something in my rectum. When he prescribed it, I was recovering from a migraine that could have been measured on the Richter scale. But even in the face of incessant throbbing and waves of nausea, pain is still preferable to sodomy.

I make it to bed somewhere between seven and ten and manage to fall asleep. The initial pain subsides and my appetite returns. Although still nauseous, the thought of a bowl of oatmeal is appealing until I see a letter from MCI Shirley on the kitchen table approving my request to visit Dad and Kev, who was moved after serving four years on the permanent work force in Concord.

My appetite shrivels with resurging nausea. In the morning, Grandma paces the downstairs, checking and rechecking her outfit. "Those sons of bitches check every goddamn thing, and if one hair is out of place, they won't let you in," she mutters mid-pace.

Breakfast is made with the same reluctance as dressing. The unmade bed pleads for me to return to it for the day. Grandma hands me a list. "Make sure you read this. Those bastards will look for any excuse to turn you away." She hands it to me and storms off to recheck her outfit. "Would you believe those S.O.B's bring me into a separate room to search my wig?" And then she whispers, "*And my bra*. I'm an old lady for Christ's sake. What the hell am I going to put up there?"

I listen with one ear while scanning the paper she handed me listing the dress code and visiting room rules.

The following items are NOT ALLOWED to be worn by any visitor adult or child:

- Boots worn above the knee (exception – boots below the knee will be permitted October 15 – April 15).
- Work boots will never be permitted.
- Bare feet.
- Bathing suits, shorts, any clothing with excessive pockets, metal, drawstrings, excessively baggy or tight clothing, hooded clothing, sheer, excessively revealing or transparent

clothing, bodysuits of any type or wrap around shirts. (Children age 8 and younger may wear shorts.)

- With the exception of undergarments, spandex or spandex type clothing is not allowed.

- Any clothing that displays a gang affiliation or is in any way attributable to gang culture; additionally, clothing that is obscene, racist or displays sexual content is not allowed.

- Any clothing similar to that issued to an inmate or uniformed personnel to include nursing scrubs, police, postal and utility. (Class A active military uniforms are allowed.)

- Fatigue or camouflage clothing.

- Double layered clothing on the bottom half of their person (e.g. two (2) pairs of pants, or skirt and slacks, etc.).

- Bibbed clothing of any type: shorts, dress, pants, overalls, jumper, etc. (allowable for age 8 and younger).

- Hair accessories that cannot be easily removed to be searched.

- Bobby pins, barrettes, and ribbons. .

- Umbrellas, jackets, coats, vests, or outerwear of any type. Exceptions can be made for those facilities where visitors have to travel outside to get to the visiting area. An area will be designated to store/hang these items not accessible to the visitor and inmate during the visit.

- Male visitors cannot wear any type of blue or black jeans into a facility that houses males. Female visitors cannot wear any type of blue or black jeans into a facility that houses females.

- Earrings, facial/body jewelry, necklaces, bracelets, and watches are not allowed. The only exception regarding jewelry is a traditional engagement ring/wedding band, religious medallion, and medical alert jewelry.
- Dresses, skirts and skirt slits will not exceed 2" above the knee when sitting. No wrap-around style skirts are allowed unless worn for religious reasons.
- Tank tops, halter tops, muscle shirts, or clothing that reveals the midriff or excessively exposes the back. Tube tops of any type are not allowed. Sleeveless clothing is not allowed unless covered by an article of clothing, such as a sweater, that shall not be removed.
- Sweatshirts, sweatpants, wind pants, and exercise clothing (allowable for age 8 and younger).
- Clothing with zippers that go the full length of the garment with the exception of outerwear (allowable for age 8 and younger).
- Colored T-shirts are allowed in. T-shirts with offensive logos are not allowed.
- Leg warmers.
- Hats and head coverings of any type, unless worn for religious or medical reasons; however they must be searched prior to entering the institution.

- No electronic communication devices or those capable of storing information are allowed.

I read as both a former inmate, cognizant of the fact that each rule is written because of assholes trying to find a way to smuggle contraband, and as a citizen, glad Shirley, and the policies that govern it, exists.

I barely sleep. Grandma squawks from the bottom stair, "We'll need to get going if we expect to be in the first wave." I rise and get dressed, weary already and I haven't even made it out the door.

Over an hour's drive west of the city, civilization dwindles to random farms and occasional warehouses. The road in is tree-lined, barren, and badly paved. Visitors aren't allowed to wait in the prison parking lot, so early birds have to park on the access road until noon. The first one checked in is the first one called to the visiting room, so the rush to the window has the potential to get ugly: Moms, grandmas, dads, and granddads all pushing and shoving to be first in line.

A guard opens the window a few minutes past noon. Second in line, Grandma slides her ID, followed my mine and the approved letter from the superintendent, through the hole in the bottom of the window. He looks the letter over and asks, "How long ago were you an inmate here?"

"More than a year ago," I reply.

He disappears from sight and comes back with the sergeant, who says I can come in but we can't all sit together. No explanation is offered.

"Why?" Grandma asks, a hint of bitchiness in her tone.

"You need approval from the superintendent," he replies.

"But we have permission," she adds.

"Not to see them both."

"Can't you make an exception?" she asks.

"No."

Forty-five minutes later, they call us. We're led into a small room with a metal detector and told to remove our shoes, socks, and belts. A male guard pats me down while a female brings Grandma into the adjacent room to search her bra and wig. Then they lead us into the prison. The building seems immune to fading, which leaves little doubt that prison coerced the elements to abandon their usual fodder and pass over the place lightly, adding to the feeling that, once inside, all time ceases.

Preceding fences are only buzzed open after the current gate is locked. The outside of the visiting room building is adorned with flowers that are pale and listless, bent as if weighed down. The deodorant I applied this morning is no match for the stench of stress that rises from my every pore.

The guard seats us on opposite sides of the room and lets us know that, under no circumstances, are we to communicate with anyone but the inmate approved by the sergeant. I'm happy to get

Kevin. In the past four years, I've only talked to Kev or Dad over the phone.

Then I see Dad. I dissected a baby pig in biology that formaldehyde had preserved, but there was no mistaking its passing, no mistaking that the beast was stone dead. I don't liken Dad to that dead baby pig, but the comparison persists in terms of preservation, with a marked difference. The pig was preserved dead, Dad while still alive. Knowing him, Dad will probably live exactly twelve years past his expiration date.

In black jeans, a white T, and a denim button down, Dad nods hello as he walks across the room to greet Grandma. Kev hands off his pass to the guard at the desk and scans the room, a put-out look on his face. "Why the fuck can't we sit together?" he asks.

"It's good to see ya. I'm fine, thanks."

"That's fucking stupid. What the fuck is the difference whether or not we sit together? What do they care?" I note that he chooses this course in lieu of a hug and warm greeting.

"And all the bitching and moaning will help how?" I ask, unsure if it's the question that gets him to stop or the fact that 'bitching and moaning' was what Mom used to say. "Here. I got you some sandwiches," I add, trying to appease him.

Watching him eat is tantamount to watching a shark feed. There is no enjoyment, just the assimilation of calories. "So what's up with the house?" he asks once an adequate number of calories have been consumed.

I shrug. "Nothing. I guess I never realized how much money it took to run a house, even if it's paid for."

"What about the insurance money," he asks, referring to the money I received from Mom's work, which equaled a year of her salary, a whopping fifteen grand.

"Well, seven of it went to pay the funeral home, another seven went to pay outstanding property taxes, and the rest is going to the phone company because calls from prison aren't cheap." The last comment ensures Kev doesn't call for a month.

"Should we sell it?" he asks.

I shrug. "What do you think?"

He shrugs. "We should ask Dad."

"You can ask Dad."

"I will. Maybe we should keep it."

"And how do we pay the twenty-five hundred dollar property tax bill every year, plus utilities, plus expenses?"

"We could rent it out."

"Me, a landlord? What if some shitbags rent it out and trash the place? Or better yet, what if something goes wrong with the roof or the plumbing. I can't fix that stuff."

"I just don't think we should sell it. Equity is like gold we can borrow against anytime we want," he says.

"Anything we borrow we have to pay back, and right now, another lien is coming unless I pay the first half of this year's tax bill. The only reason I could see us keeping it is if one or both of us were thinking of living there. Are you?"

He nods no. "Dad says property is the best investment. Too bad we couldn't keep it until he gets out. Then we could redo the whole house and sell it for twice what it's worth now."

The idea makes me nauseous. Growing up, Dad bought a house thirty miles west of the suburbs in a town called Groton. He paid to have the foundation poured on five acres, capped it, and lived there while he framed, dry-walled, and finished the house. I came to know weekends as labor camp. Just the thought of the experience caused migraines every Thursday. A weekend filled with Dad and Kev belittling my meager appetite and meek frame.

"We can't wait eight more years. By then there'll be so many liens on the house the government will take it," I argue.

"Just sell it then, I guess." He shrugs. The sleeves of his triple X shirt become taut.

I lean forward to telegraph the gravity of my next question. "Do you blame him at all?"

"Who? Dad? No," is all he offers.

"How can you not?"

"You're an adult. You didn't have to rob anyone. You should've said no when we asked."

I feel foolish for expecting more than a cut-and-dried response. "I guess."

"Count is in fifteen minutes. If you don't want to stay through count, you need to leave now!" is announced.

"You guys should go," Kev says.

We walk out, me ahead of Grandma and rushing to the car. She is silent on the way home. Her hand gestures suggest an internal conversation, thinking ahead to the letter she'll write to the superintendent requesting permission for us all to sit together.

Bob

Thanksgiving comes. I've been at my new job as an assistant manager at Gold's Gym now for a few months and offer to work to avoid spending it in the prison visiting room, but instead we go on my day off. There's no escaping it. A letter given to the guard from the superintendent grants us permission to sit together, and for the first time in years, we sit as a family.

"It's good to see you, son," Dad says as he hugs me.

"You too, Dad."

"How's school going?" He says this after sitting. Kev tears open the first of three sandwiches, and Grandma looks as happy as I've seen her in months.

"Fine. I graduate in a month."

"That's great, son. Then what? Think you'll stay in this job for awhile?'

"Not sure," I answer.

"Oh, he's doing just great," Grandma adds. "They pay his health insurance and he started a savings account." She is beaming.

"Wow, son. It sounds like things are going well."

"Yeah, great."

"Your brother says you're thinking of selling the house."

"Mmm-hmm."

"Is that the best idea?" He is baiting me. Clearly he has an opinion, one discussed with all parties present, save me, prior.

I shrug.

"The best advice I can give you is that real estate is a precious commodity. Take it from me, I've bought and paid for several houses in my life and there's nothing like it. You can make some real money if you're smart about it."

His inclusion in a decision intended for heirs only pisses me off. Kev sits like he did in court, letting his lawyer do the talking. If Dad suggested burning it for the insurance, he'd be the first to spread the accelerant and light the match.

"And being smart includes what?" I ask, wondering if he's implying what I think he's implying.

"Well, equity is liquidity. It takes some people years to accrue that kind of capital. You two could borrow from it anytime you need to, and with interest rates going down, it's not a bad idea to hold on to the house."

"And who'll pay the upkeep?" I ask.

"You could try to save for that. You're making decent money now. Just keep a running tab and pay yourself back after it's sold."

"Uh-huh. I'm hungry. I'm going to get something to eat." I get up and shuffle between the seat and Kev's tree trunk legs.

They huddle while I'm gone, conspiring. I find the click of the right arrow that moves the turnstile of choices in the vending machine soothing. Grandma recaps the discussion on the way home, adding that she approves of Dad's idea and offers to pay the taxes. The next day, I make appointments with realtors to assess the house.

The next day, with the taste of bile still lingering in my throat after the visit with Dad, I get out of bed and grab a phone book out of the five or six stacked in the closet and look under therapists. I look for ads that might reveal the type of clinician I'm looking for. A therapist who sits and nods empathetically, occasionally asking how something makes me feel, won't cut it. I need someone to challenge me. Bob's ad stands out: *Are you looking for real feedback? Want a therapist that can make a difference, who will collaborate with you to solve real life problems? I can.* I leave a message at two a.m. and he calls me first thing in the morning. We set an appointment for later that afternoon.

I leave work a few hours early and call him when I can't find his office. "Gee, you must be excited to get started — you're three hours early."

"I was going to get coffee first. I just wanted to make sure I knew where you were located."

He's in an office atop a row of stores. I climb the stairs apprehensively. Low wattage bulbs bathe the waiting room in soft light. I distract myself by making the tea made available to clients on a table near the door. I note that white noise machines staggered along the hallway discourage would-be eavesdroppers. Bob emerges from the office at the end of the hall. He's gangly with small rimmed glasses butted firmly on the bridge of his nose. Wearing khakis and an untucked, slightly disheveled, flannel button down, he extends his hand. "Hello, Bryan. I'm Bob."

"Nice to meet you."

"Come down to my office."

The room is plain. A small couch and armchair sit opposite what I surmise to be Bob's seat. I contemplate taking it to see how he'll interpret the choice, but then I decide on the couch. He sits, shuts off his cell, and folds his hands neatly on his lap.

"Where should I start?"

"Like I told you on the phone, I believe it is useful for prospective clients to evaluate a prospective therapist at no charge. This isn't a free therapy session, but a chance to see the office, meet me, and ask questions that will help you decide if I'm someone you want to work with. I won't be interviewing you — I'm the one on the spot. It's isn't the only opportunity for you to ask questions, however. You are welcome to ask questions and get answers at any time during your therapy as well."

"I've been to tons of therapists, but I never interviewed one before."

He shrugs. "I see myself as a consultant hired by someone to work on their particular goals. I believe everyone has a healthy part of their psyche; therefore, you will be treated as an intelligent, collaborative partner in the therapeutic process. I'll treat you with respect and compassion because I believe all people are respect-worthy. My approach is down-to-earth and realistic, free of mystical or evasive thinking and behavior. I'm not managerial, but at the same time, I am far from passive. I answer questions openly, occasionally give advice and recommendations, and suggest efficient ways of using your sessions. I encourage free speech, and I treat, with interest and respect, any questions, comments, or criticisms you may have, including angry ones."

"So I'm supposed to ask you questions?"

"Anything you want to know." He nods.

"Okay. Where'd you go to school?"

"I studied computer software at The University of Massachusetts, took some psychology classes and was introduced to my good friend and mentor, Jacob Gill, the founder of the Psychotherapy Institute, where I've studied for five years." His self assuredness borders on superiority. I think he is skating on leeway he only has on loan at the moment.

"The Institute? Never heard of it. This is a school?" I ask.

"It is in the sense that we all study and learn through our own therapy with Jacob. We attend group counseling as well as

individual. After five years of study, we're allowed to practice."
He then sips tea from a Dixie cup.

A period of silence ensues. I'm at a loss for words. I want
to get up and leave, but ultimately I stay, asking, "Can we get
started?"

Bob's raised eyebrow has a gotcha quality that makes me
wince. "Well, it's a quarter past. Did you want to prorate the rest of
the hour and pay me $45 for the rest of your scheduled time?"

"Fine with me," I say, anxious to rattle off my list of
traumas.

He readjusts, sitting straighter, like a beacon ready to
receive. I wait for instructions, but none come and so I just begin:
"I was raised by an alcoholic, my mom, recently deceased. I spent
the last few months of her life taking care of her. She used to beat
us, my older brother and me. She divorced my father when we
were very young, and she told me recently that he used to beat me,
not my brother, when I was a kid. I remember him grabbing me by
the hair, lifting me, and tossing me into a wall, all because I
touched a stain glass window he was painting. While he and my
mother were having marital problems, just before the divorce, I'd
wake up to him in my bed snuggling me. Once, he hugged me too
tight. When I woke him up to complain, he threw me into a
dresser. My brother and mother both remember other incidents that
I don't. Both confirm I was thrown down the stairs." I pause to let
it sink in. Bob appears unshaken by the outpouring, and so I
continue. "I hate my father." At this Bob raises an eyebrow. "My

mother died of cancer. I took care of her, alone, for the last few months of her life. Prior to that, I was in prison. My father, brother, and I robbed jewelry stores all over New England for five years." I wait to see what he does with it.

"Sounds like you've had quite a life."

"I'll say."

"Your parents sound really sick."

"My father is an asshole," I snap.

Bob places his closed hand under his chin with his index finger extended along the side of his narrow face. "Well, I believe there are no assholes in that metaphorical sense you are using the term."

"What?

"I believe there are no assholes in the world, only sick people. Sounds like your dad and mom fall into that category. I believe there are no bad people, only people with greater or lesser degrees of mental health."

"That's interesting, but you never met my dad."

"True, but it does us no good to go around thinking that there are good and bad people."

"So there are no assholes?" I confirm.

"No."

"Hitler wasn't an asshole?"

Bob raises the same eyebrow. "Power corrupts, as they say, and absolute power corrupts absolutely. Hitler was an abused child, and abused children abuse others."

"So my dad isn't an asshole?"

"A question we'll explore in depth, I'm sure."

I leave, uncomfortable with his interpretation but vow to return, if only to prove his theory wrong. I know for a fact that Dad is an asshole.

With the house now on the market, I think about the arduous task of packing everything up. It's easier to compartmentalize than to attack the project holistically. I think of each room as a separate entity. I intend to sell the lacquered bedroom set and a few oddball pieces of furniture in the spare bedroom to the first person who wants it. The kitchen, I'll yard sale. The old, pressed cardboard wall units in the living room will go to the dump. The antique dining room table is promised to my aunt, who says she will send a truck. I avoid sentimentality's snare by ignoring Mom's room and the basement, where boxes of forget-me-nots are stored.

With Kevin's opposition to the sale noted and dismissed, I haul boxes to Grandma's for the estate sale I advertised in the local paper. The ad clearly states that the sale is to start at eight a.m., but people knock on the door at quarter to six and some called the night before and asked to come early. It's astounding how many people show up and offer to buy things that aren't for sale, like Grandma's lawn decorations and empty buckets she uses for weeds. She sells anything they ask to buy and I am cleaned out of my mother's stuff before ten. The boxes I hauled the stuff here in look like carcasses picked clean. Years of history are reduced to a wad of bills stuffed into a glass cup. I retire to my room, lie down, and fall fast asleep.

Grandma wakes me, frantic. "The money is missing."

"What?" I ask, blinking the grog away.

"Get up. Oh my god. The money is missing." She paces, pulling apart the room.

I say, "It's got to be here somewhere. I'll find it later," and I roll over, hoping she'll leave.

"I said, get up! Now! What if someone took it?"

I sit. "I think I put it in one of the boxes while I was cleaning up."

"Find it!" she snaps.

I pull apart empty boxes, sure that's where I left the glass. Grandma looms like a storm cloud threatening a picnic. Alas, I find it at the bottom of one of the boxes.

"Got it!" I yell.

Grandma's neck muscles unclench. "You found it?"

"Yup," I reply, like a kid brandishing a near perfect report card.

"Oh my god," she says with her hand on her chest. "What if we lost all that money?"

"We didn't. I just misplaced it, temporarily," I joke.

She sneers and says, "You've never learned."

"Learned what?"

"I've spent my whole life trying to teach you kids about money, and you've never learned," she hisses. "You flaunt what you don't have. Without me, you'd all be poor. It's because I scrimp and save every penny that all of you aren't in the poorhouse."

"Geez, relax. I have the money."

"You have that money!" she screams. "But what about the money for the lawyer, or the money I sent for canteen, or the money for the TV you needed when you were away! What about that! Where do you think that came from?"

"You. I know that."

"You don't know anything! I grew up in the Depression. We had nothing! No food, no shoes. We worked, all us kids. No one lounged around. My mother taught us the power of money. How if you don't have it, you're nothing!"

"Calm down." She's as heated as I've ever seen, but this time is completely different from the handful of times she's gone off in the past. She is not merely bitching, but focused, her anger a stick she is hell-bent on breaking across my back.

"No!" She stomps her foot as she says the word. "You don't see me gallivanting around, do you? No, I stay home and watch every nickel for you kids, and for your father too. You've all taken advantage of my frugalness while you run around like kings."

Feeling as if I had enough berating, I fight back. "Where do you think we learned it, huh? You threw money at us our whole lives. I've never walked out of here without a pocket full of cash, and half the time, I didn't ask for it."

"And what did you do? You went out and bought drugs with it!" Her eyes bulge. "You never turned it down because you like living like a king. Eighty dollar sneakers, hundred dollar jackets. 'Oh, look at me! I'm a king!' But you never once learned to put it away, to save, like me. That's what I tried to teach you kids: if you have money, people treat you like a king, and if you don't, you're nothing to them! And what thanks do I get for all my hard work? Your father goes out and robs people. I can't go to the grocery store without seeing someone who asks me how my son is, and do you know what I have to do? I have to lie. I'm supposed to be enjoying my golden years, surrounded by family. Instead I have to be strip searched to see them!"

She storms off in a huff. My feet remain glued to the floor because I know she'll be back. "You misplace money like it's worthless. But let me tell you, without it you're shit. Hear me? I know what it's like to be poor and have people look down at you like you're scum. Money makes kings and poverty makes you a third class citizen. What made your father do it? Was it a girl? Some woman must have gotten into his head and made him do what he did. He'd never have done it on his own. Why? Tell me why." Deep crevices in her face reveal the level of her perplexity over the question she has posed.

"I wish I knew."

The conversation ends with her going to lie down. I peek in on her to make sure she's okay. Her wig is slung over the back of the chair near the pullout bed. Her snore echoes through the house.

I meet with Bob every Friday, and so Saturday through Thursday I hope something comes up in my life that will soak up the majority of the hour with him. Grandma's explosion provides just such an opportunity. I find Bob in his usual seat, a Dixie cup of tea placed carefully on the tiny table next to his chair. The shades are open; the vegetation beyond flourishes. Between the branches, I see a house and wonder what dynamic exists behind its walls. That thought distracts me even while I reiterate the weekend's events for him.

"What were you feeling while she yelled at you?" he asks.

"Feeling? I was pissed at first, even fought back a little, but then I stood there and let her unleash on me. It's typical really, for her anyway. She just holds it all inside, and then she explodes at inopportune moments.'

"So you got angry initially?"

"Well, yeah. She was screaming at me."

"But why get angry?"

"I don't know. She pissed me off. She was so mad about something that was nothing — I had the money."

"You think this was about the money?" Bob asks.

"Don't you?"

"I don't know. That's why it's important to help me with as many of the details as you can remember. What were you feeling, where were you standing, were you scared, annoyed, frustrated, sad? Theses are made of the rich details that will help me help you."

"All I can really remember about what I was feeling was that I was angry. I wanted to lash back at her, and I did, sort of. Dad always told us to just let her scream, that she'd be fine if she just got whatever was bothering her off her chest."

"And how do you understand your anger?" Bob asks.

"What do you mean, how do I understand it?"

"I mean, what is your understanding of the emotion?"

"I'm not sure I understand it." I slouch as if backing away.

"I think it's important to come to an understanding of what anger is and what it's isn't so that you can express it, get it out of the way, and reveal what's behind it."

The room grows eerily quiet. To break the silence, I blurt, "Help me out here. I feel like you're waiting for me to say something, but I'm waiting for you to tell me what the hell you mean. Anger is anger. How the fuck do I come to an understanding?"

"Maybe we should explore how you're feeling right now."

"I'm pissed! Why do you do that?" I ask from the edge of the sofa.

"Do what?" Bob asks.

"Look, I know you're leading me somewhere, so let's cut the crap. Just tell me what you mean."

"You mean you want me to do the work for you."

I hold one of the couch pillows like a life preserver. "No, I don't want you to do the work for me. I just don't know what you want me to say."

"Let's talk about your depression."

"My depression? I'm not depressed."

"Really? If I had a camera and took a snapshot of you, what do you think it would look like?" Bob asks.

"Hell if I know."

"Take a look at yourself now," he says.

I notice how far I've sunk into the corner of the couch. "I see your point," I admit reluctantly.

"How clearly can we see things when we're all balled up like that?"

"Not very."

"It's these times, times we are stressed, angry, that it's important to sit up, look around, and realize where you are. Remind yourself that you're in no danger. You're safe, just like you were standing in that kitchen. There was no real threat. So why get so angry?"

"I don't know. It's automatic, I guess."

"Anger is a non-optional response to pain, a process of evolution designed to protect us from the threat of physical harm. In the absence of bodily harm, anger is neurotic. What you need to ask is: why am I hurt?"

My gaze never leaves the window. To look at Bob would release the floodgates. "So, who hurt you?" he asks.

"Everyone," I respond.

"Got any specifics, or did you intend on being so vague?"

"No, I mean everyone," I say, now turning my gaze to look right into him.

"I wonder how well you see reality while you're depressed."

"I'm not depressed, damn it! I agree that I'm angry, but I am not depressed."

"Okay, so everyone hurt you?"

"Yes, everyone hurt me."

"I'm quite sure I haven't," he says with conviction. "Would you agree?"

"Yeah."

"That's what I mean. These emotionally charged times are when it's most important to make sure you can see reality clearly. Your neurotic side wants you to believe everyone hurt you, but is that the reality of your life?"

"No."

"Then who?"

"My father."

"How?"

"He's the reason I went to prison."

"He hurt you long before that," Bob interjects.

"I guess. I've always struggled to connect with him, but I never understood him."

"If you want to know what makes your father tick, you have to figure out what makes her tick."

"Who?"

"His mother."

"I know the answer to that: money."

"Sounds like a good guess," Bob says with a smile. "But it's not just currency itself that gave birth to her neurotic side. It's a false belief about money that fuels her behavior. That's what we do here, try to uncover your false beliefs, drag them into the light and examine them. You developed them for a reason. They helped you survive as a defenseless child in a dangerous home. But they don't serve you well anymore, just like they don't serve your grandmother. I believe that, if she had a firmer grasp of reality, she would realize that she could lose everything and she'd still be okay."

"I guess," I say.

"I'll see you next week," Bob says as I get up to go.

"Sure thing."

The urge to run, jump, and frolic after my boss at Gold's offers me the general manager position at their new club, is overwhelming. But an intense feeling of inadequacy causes me to call Bob and ask if he's available for an appointment.

"What makes you think you'll fail?" Bob asks, who fit me in after a cancellation.

"A hunch. Let's face it. Things haven't gone according to plan thus far."

"I'm not a huge believer in hunches. I am, however, a believer in determinants."

"Explanation please."

"All thoughts, feelings, and behaviors are caused or forced by one's set of unique determinants. Science proves that every experience hardwires our brains, so if a child is struck by Mom, that experience leaves more than a mark — it determines how they'll react to future experiences. A determinant is something that has a role in causing, or determining, an outcome. For example, heat is the significant determinant in forcing something to boil. Every action has an equal and opposite reaction."

"What about free will?"

"An illusion," he answers like a lawyer expecting the question.

"So there's no free will?"

"It's likely that childhood traumas have a lasting effect on the unconscious. Those unconscious memories may be stirred up by present day situations and have an effect on our feelings, thoughts and behaviors, effects that in most cases may be unknown to the person experiencing them. These factors are not within our control, and they are certainly not the result of our own deliberate actions. If this is the case, then how can there be free will?"

"That makes sense, I guess," I say.

"Think of yourself as a scientist. The scientific method requires us to gather evidence in order to support theories. Beliefs are like theories. We can't ever know if our beliefs are absolutely correct. All we can do is gather evidence that either backs or refutes our beliefs." He folds his hands on his lap after swilling the last of his tea. "So what's got you so provoked about this new job?"

"The worry that I'll screw it up," I answer.

"And what kind of person screws up such a great opportunity?"

"An asshole."

"So you're an asshole?" he asks.

"I must be."

"From what you know about the owners, do they typically put assholes in charge of new clubs?"

"They do now," I snap.

"Hmm. I wonder where the evidence is that you're an asshole."

"Evidence?"

"Yeah, evidence. You must be able to produce some evidence to back up the belief that you're an asshole."

"Look at me! Have you heard anything I've said? I'm shit!"

"So Gold's hires shit?"

"No. I guess not. Not usually. Maybe I just slipped under the radar."

"Do you think the owners are secretly trying to bankrupt the business?" Bob snickers at his own craftiness.

"Look, I get it, but I still don't believe it."

"What, that you're not an asshole?"

"Yes."

Bob's snicker persists. "Then present your evidence."

"I have none."

"Then in the absence of evidence…" Bob lets me fill in the rather large hole.

"I get it."

"I'm trying, Bryan, to get you to see that the tape playing in your head telling you you're shit, that you're unworthy and undeserving, is spinning lies. You believe in lies. None of what you said is reality, and when we can't see reality, we can't see a damned thing. If you pick your head up and look around and remind yourself I'm okay, there's no danger here. Even if I do screw up, lose my job, and the gym goes belly up, I'm going to be fine."

"It doesn't feel that way."

"Clearly. Let's talk about that then."

"What?" I ask.

"How you feel." Bob places his open hands on his knees. My eyes dart around the room trying to make it look as though they happen upon the clock by chance. Fifteen minutes left.

"I don't know," I reply, hating his stare. "I'm angry."

"Sounds like you're guessing."

"How the fuck should I know how I feel?"

"Now you sound angry." Bob shifts in his seat.

"Fuck this."

"Fuck what? Therapy?"

"Everything," I say.

"How do you understand your anger, Bryan?"

"I don't."

"What purpose does it serve?" He is baiting me, but I think, what the hell? I'll play.

"None that I can see."

"I believe anger is a non-optional response to pain. So the question that begs answering is: why are you hurt?"

"Isn't it obvious?" I ask.

"What is of paramount importance is its expression. Anger is like toxic waste: no one wants it dumped near them. If you can express it, grit your teeth and kick and scream in here, then you're less likely to dump it out there."

"I'll try," I say, already halfway to the door.

"Remember when I asked you to move my retirement fund out of Scientific Devices?" Dad asks after I accept the charges and we exchange pleasantries.

"I do," I answer.

"They just sent me a letter from the accounting department. It turns out they miscalculated, and they're sending me another six grand."

"I see. At least they calculated in your favor." I joke.

"True. Anyway, I've decided to give the money to you and your brother to split. Kevin says you can have his half until he gets out if you need it."

"That's very generous. Thank you."

"No problem, son. I just wish it could be more."

Me too, I think, but I don't say it. "No, it's more than enough. Thanks again."

Grandma hands me a check the next day for the six grand and I immediately take it to the bank, put it into my checking, and drive my 1981 Ford Thunderbird straight to the nearest Nissan dealership and buy a Nissan Xterra.

I've never had a brand new car before, especially one that promises a life full of adventure now that I can slip into four wheel drive and scale walls.

Pulling into the garage, I take out a fresh micro-fiber cloth from the pack of twenty and wipe down the entire truck, inside and out. I snap a few pictures and notice spots around the front wheel hub that require extensive wiping.

Inside is a message from the realtor that another offer was made on the house, a hundred and nineteen thousand. I accept. When Kev calls, I let him know the news.

"So we're not going to keep it?" he asks.

"No," I answer.

"Big mistake, Bry."

"Maybe. What do you want me to do with your share?"

"Put in Fidelity with Dad's," he says.

"You get out soon. Are you excited?" I ask just to change topics.

"Why?"

"Why? How can you ask that? Do you like it there?"

"Honestly, after eight years, I'm used to it. Besides, what's waiting for me out there?"

I forgo a list of reasons, knowing how selective Kev's hearing is. "At least you'll have a little nest egg, thanks to Mom."

"For what? I mean, what am I going to do?"

"Anything you want," I answer, knowing he faces an uphill battle.

"Dude, I have several violent felonies on my record, and I've been away for eight years. Who the hell is going to hire me?"

"I got hired," I say, though we have had this very conversation many times before.

"You're different," he says, expecting it.

"How am I different?"

"You only did three years," he says, obliterating any hint that I struggled to get on with life after my release.

"Right," I say, ready to wrap this conversation up. "Well, maybe we'll open our own gym." I immediately wish for the ability to inhale the words back.

"Yeah, where?"

"Anywhere." I answer.

"Florida."

"It's competitive there, hell anywhere. You'd have to lose about thirty pounds."

"Lose? I was thinking I'd gain a few," he says, already tipping the scales at two fifty.

"And scare any potential members away? Listen, the age of the meathead is over. Misconceptions already keep people from going to the gym, and the last thing we need is to pander to meatballs who have no loyalty to the club. Women over forty, dude, that's the market, that's who spends money on training and group exercise. Meatheads are a dime a dozen."

"Well, I'm not running some namby-pamby girlie club. I want a power lifting gym with squat racks and dead lifting platforms."

"Well, I'm not interested in opening a prison gym."

"Then me and Dad will open a powerhouse and you can open a froufrou girlie gym."

"Fine," I say, and hear the word come back at me just before the click.

Walking down the hall elicits a feeling I can't escape. If early, I wait till the last second. Mostly, I'm a few minutes late. He always waits in his chair with a full Dixie cup of tea. I look for variances in his appearance, something that tells me he doesn't sit here all week, that he actually exists outside this realm. There aren't any.

He never says a word until I do. No greeting even. I say hello to break whatever tension I've created. He answers back in an even tone, "Hello, Bryan."

There is no preamble or recap of last week's session. I am always encouraged to think about what I want to work on, and so I start with my current crisis. "I'm worried about my brother getting out."

"When is that?" Bob asks.

"Next week."

"Why are you worried?"

"I don't know. It's been a long time since he was out, since we were together. I'm ashamed to say that sometimes I'm more comfortable with him in there than out here." It is an admission I regret as soon as it comes out.

"Ashamed? That is a pretty powerful word," Bob says. "Why shame?"

"Because I shouldn't feel that way," I say with an air of snippiness, hating to state the obvious and knowing he'll pick it apart.

"But you do. We should examine that, don't you think?"

"No, but you do."

"It's important, Bryan, because guilt is a great motivator, possibly the greatest. Depending on the intensity, it makes us behave in ways we otherwise wouldn't."

"Like robbing jewelry stores?" I smirk at him.

"Now you're thinking like a scientist. So what is it that's so provocative about your brother getting out?"

"We have a tumultuous past. He stands out in my mind as the greatest bully in history. He tortured me as a kid." I slouch, drawing inward.

"Got any details?" Bob asks.

"There was never any rest when he was around. Even when he wasn't, I felt him lurking. He made it a point to terrorize me when we were kids and he never relented. Mom would put us to bed early so she could drink, and I remember one night he stood up on his bed and jumped off, hitting the ground with a thud because he knew she'd come up the stairs with the paddle. She beat us both pretty good, despite my insistence I had nothing to do with it. When she left, he got up again. I said, 'She's gonna beat you too.' He looked at me and said, 'I don't care. It's worth it to watch you get beat.'"

"Take a second to look at yourself," Bob says. "What do you think you look like right now?"

I'm on the edge of the seat, back straight as a board, leaning forward. "Looks good on you," Bob adds.

"What?"

"Your anger looks good."

"What the fuck does that mean?"

"It means congrats on letting it spill in here instead of out there where it does real harm."

"Thanks, I guess."

"Like I said, anger is like toxic waste — no one likes it dumped near them. But it demands expression. I suspect that all your troubles at work stem from an inability to express your anger in a healthy way, like you just did. It leaks out at inopportune times."

"I get it."

"Great. Now let's examine this guilt of yours. Why do you feel so responsible for what your brother does, or doesn't do, when he gets out?"

"Because I promised her I'd take care of him," I whisper.

"Your mom…" He both states and asks when he says it.

"She made me promise. She was on her deathbed and made me promise repeatedly that I'd take care of him," I say, tears flowing freely.

"Did you discuss what that looks like?" Bob asks.

"What do you mean?"

"I mean, were there details beyond a vague promise?"

"No. I know what she meant."

"Care to elaborate?" he asks.

"She meant for me to look out for him and make sure he's okay."

"Does that mean you are to peek in on him while he's sleeping or does that mean to clothe, bath, and feed him?"

I shrug.

"Unfortunate," Bob adds.

"Why? Haven't you ever taken care of anyone?"

Here he contemplates as if deciding how much to share. "If you're asking me if I've made promises I couldn't keep, then yes."

"What makes you think I can't keep it?" I ask.

"Oh, I have no doubt you'll die trying, such is the danger in deathbed promises. But I submit to you that no one can take care of another in the sense that you can't change his mind, can't make him eat right, can't make him sleep enough, and can't make him stay sober. You can suggest all you want, but such behavior is self-serving." Bob points out a box of tissues on the table.

I pull two out and ask, "What do you mean, self-serving?"

"What I mean is that one hundred percent of all human behavior is selfish."

"How does that work?" I ask in disbelief.

"If I sell all my worldly possessions, move to Africa, and donate to the poor, I do so for the way it makes me feel, nothing else.

"Jesus Christ. Let me get this straight: there are no assholes, anger is a non-optional response to pain, and now all selfless behavior is selfish?"

Bob smirks, obviously about to declare checkmate. "Precisely, since you can never truly be without the self?" And just like someone who has been checkmated, I relent. "This is the reason we should avoid making deathbed promises. Because now that she's gone, how will you ever know when that promise to her is fulfilled? Your mother made you promise something that's impossible, and for that, I am sorry."

Wrapped-up

It's a strange feeling, picking someone up from prison. I doubt Mom felt the same apprehension when she picked me up, however. Grandma sits shotgun, glad she didn't have to fight the wild horses it would have taken to prevent her presence.

My truck is freshly waxed and the inside gleams, the leather washed with saddle soap for a second time in two months. I notice a streak of Armor-all on one of the alloy rims and buff it out before going in. In typical prison fashion, we wait for an hour before Kev emerges from the same door we go in to visit. The aura of freeness I expect isn't there, only the same stench of apprehension. I know how he feels, as if he'll be snatched up again, a feeling that persists for months. Dreams of being back in will permeate every sleep.

"Nice truck," he says, straining the shocks with his massive frame.

Grandma insists on riding in the back. Kev immediately turns on the AC. "Thanks," I reply.

"How's work?" he asks.

"Mind numbing," I answer.

"That sucks," he says, scanning through radio stations and scoffing at my choice of presets.

"I'm so glad you're out, darling," Grandma shouts from the back.

Kev grunts.

We make our way toward probation so he can check in, then wait at an emergency room for four hours so he can get a script for needles and insulin. When I drop my grandmother and brother off, Kev asks, "Where you going?"

"I moved out a week ago so you could have the upstairs to yourself."

A weight lifts off the shocks, and off my mind, when they exit. I cruise back to Salem to the comforts of my one bedroom apartment. It's small but right near Salem's downtown. The location is nostalgic. I spent my childhood downtown. Every July fourth, Mom brought us to watch the fireworks. The Willows, a boardwalk of arcades, junk food, and rides is just a half mile away.

Living alone is the freest I've ever felt, paying rent and utilities a joy. Money is tight. But I wouldn't trade a second here for all the savings in the world if it meant I had to move back to Grandma's.

"I want to be a trainer," Kev says.

"I know, but Gold's won't hire you to be a trainer — you're too intimidating."

"What? No I'm not."

"Dude, I know you don't believe it, but you're too big. People don't want gargantuan trainers — they're intimidating. They want to be trained by someone they can relate to."

"Bullshit. What about powerlifters?"

"Extinct," I say.

"You mean to tell me there are no high school kids that want to put on mass and be more powerful on the field?"

"Dude, I could throw a rock right now and hit three, but they're not the ones with the money to buy training." I fail to convince and our conversation ends like so many of them do, with agreeing to disagree.

I call Kev that night when I get home from work. His phone picks up, but he doesn't answer. After three tries, I realize it's him answering but that his sugar must be low again.

"Kev? Kevin, is that you?" I shout.

I can hear him giggle just as the driver announces the next stop.

"Kev, you're on the bus and you need sugar! Do you have any?" I hear the commotion of someone scrambling.

"Hello?" a voice asks in a thick foreign accent.

"Hi. Listen. The person's phone you just picked up is having a low blood sugar reaction. Can you frisk him and see if he has any candy? He needs candy."

"Frisk?" the voice asks.

"Yeah, search him, look in pockets? *Comprende?*"

I hear more commotion, then get disconnected.

"Bry," Kev says when he calls back.

"Jesus. What the hell happened?"

"Sugar," he says, groggily.

"No shit, Sherlock."

"Sugar was crazy low," he reiterates.

"Wow. You had me scared to death."

"What can I say?" he asks.

"Nothing, I guess."

"Call me tomorrow," he says before disconnecting.

"Sounds harrowing," Bob comments after hearing of my ordeals with Kev.

"An understatement," I add.

"Makes me wonder if you've given any thought as to why you feel so compelled to help him."

"I told you why."

"Ah, deathbed promises," he says.

"Yeah, but don't you think he might change?" I ask.

Bob shrugs. "I couldn't even guess."

"Maybe he will."

"I think it's important for you to keep any expectations of your brother as low as possible," he advises.

"Why?"

"Because he hasn't been the pillar of change you've hoped he'd be up to this point, and so there's no reason to believe he'll start now."

"You don't sound enthusiastic," I say.

"My enthusiasm is for you to make sure you don't set yourself up and wind up hurt," Bob says.

"You think he'll hurt me?"

"I think you're already hurt, and expectations that go unmet will only exacerbate that hurt. Where's your dad in all this?"

"It's all his fault," I snap.

"What is?"

"All of it, the reason my brother and I struggle. As far as I'm concerned, he can rot in that godforsaken shit hole."

"Is your anger at him deeper than the robberies?" he asks.

"I've never been able to connect with him. He and my brother have always had a connection I could never get in on, like a secret club. I don't get him at all."

"Well, if you want to understand a man, you have to understand his mother," Bob says.

"Grandma? She's insane." Bob has said this before but the assertion hits me like a fist every time.

"Point made then." Bob smirks.

"So you think Dad's obsession with money stems from her?" I ask, apparently on the brink of a break though.

Bob shrugs, feigning ignorance. "Makes sense, doesn't it?"

"Perfect sense. She grew up in the depression. She scrimps and saves every penny to the exclusion of spending any money on herself. She sits home all day. She doesn't drive, and since she saw how much money I made on the yard sale, she goes to church bazaars and buys stuff to then sell to someone else. She sits out in the driveway for hours and haggles over a few pennies."

"Sounds like she may have some false beliefs about money," Bob says.

"I'll say. She's always pushed it on us as kids. We never left there without a pocket full of cash. When we couldn't see her, she'd mail it. Don't get me wrong, I loved it, but I worry that I have some wrong ideas about money that need examining because of those experiences."

"We are in the perfect venue for just such an examination," Bob says, and I detect a hint of snideness in his tone.

"Do you think it would have been possible for Dad to influence us to rob if those false beliefs weren't already instilled?"

"Do you?" he asks.

I nod in the affirmative, feeling enlightened. "I think it was always an undercurrent for me growing up, the whole money-for-love thing. I used to manipulate the hell out of Mom to buy me stuff just to prove she loved me."

"Really?" Bob asks with a raised eyebrow.

"Totally. As a matter of fact, I used to try to get sick just to get her attention," I say, which is something I have not recalled in years.

"Tell me about that."

"There are two instances that come to mind, the first when I was walking to school in the first grade. My brother, who was supposed to walk me there, dumped me when we reached his friend's house. I proceeded alone and stepped out in front of a car that was speeding by."

"Sounds like an unfortunate accident," Bob comments.

"Accident? No, this was premeditated. I didn't even look — I just leapt."

"You're saying you did it on purpose?"

"Not consciously, but now that I think about it, there were probably a number of reasons I didn't look both ways. It would have gotten my brother in trouble, and it would have gotten me loads of sympathy from Mom. Being sick or hurt is one of the only times she put the bottle down to take care of us."

"And you're quite sure you did it on purpose?"

Bob's inquiry makes me worry that an affirmative might get me locked in the loony bin. "Well, I only bring it up because there were other times I tried to get sick. I had a neighbor whose cut got infected so badly he got red streak infection. He said he had to be hospitalized because, if it traveled to his heart, he was dead. So the next time I had a bad cut, I rubbed dirt in it so it would get infected like his. Is that sick?" I ask.

"It never ceases to amaze me the lengths kids will go to get Mom's love and attention," Bob answers.

"I used to ransack the first aid kit in the bathroom closet and bring ACE bandages to school."

"For the teacher's attention?" Bob asks.

"Mostly so they'd leave me alone. They were always trying to get me involved with the other kids at recess, but I just wanted to be left alone."

"And now?"

"I still just want to be left alone."

"You don't talk about having a rich social life," Bob comments.

"Because I don't."

"Why is that?"

"I prefer to be alone."

"We're all alone. We're born alone. We'll die alone. But we can choose whether or not to be lonely."

The room falls silent. One more word and I'll lose it. Bob remains stoic, refusing to break the silence I initiate. The clock ticks loudly.

"This is his fault," I whimper.

"Your father?" Bob asks.

"Yes."

"You blame him for a lot, and rightfully so, but where is your mother in all this?"

"Don't!" I snap.

"Don't what?"

"My mother was a fucking saint! It's his fault, not hers! Don't you dare lump her in with him!"

"So she's a saint and he's Satan?"

"Exactly. What's your fucking point?"

"That no one can be all one thing, and to say so is to deny your own ambivalence."

"What? Make sense, man," I say.

"You love your mom and hate your dad, but it's not an all or nothing proposition. You have to love and hate them both equally. One doesn't exist without the other. I mean, intense love is meaningless without intense hate."

"So I hate my mother." I chuckle.

"What I'm saying is that it's impossible to be all one thing. You can't feel all love or all hate. So, as I'm sure you do indeed love your mother, it stands to reason, given your history, that some part of you hates her too," Bob explains. "Just as I suspect that, as much as you claim to hate your dad right now, you love him too."

"Great thought to leave me with," I say as I stand to exit.

At home, there's an email from Kev informing me that, because he's unemployed, he needs me to make monthly payments to him for the money I borrowed to buy the truck.

"Dude, I got your email. You could've just called," I say after dialing his cell.

"I knew you were working. I need that money," he says.

"I know, but listen. Things are kind of tight now. With the truck and rent, I'm tapped out. Can you give me a little time?"

"I need that money," he answers.

"For what?"

"What do you mean for what? It's my money."

"I know, and I'm totally going to pay you, but like I said, things are tight right now, and if I pay you, I'll have to give something up, like food."

"I need it." He continues unabated in his resolve.

"Why? You have zero expenses. You live with Grandma, for Christ's sake."

"I have bills. I have to pay probation every month, and I have a cell phone and internet."

"Let's be clear: grandma pays probation and gives you an allowance. I know, or have you forgotten I used to live there? You've never lived on your own so I don't expect you to understand, but it's hard. I'm seriously broke."

"I've lived on my own!" Kev snaps.

"In Florida? Dad paid every cent of your rent and expenses, so don't make it sound like you worked for it."

"I worked my ass off," Kev growls.

"We robbed people! It's not like you worked forty hours a week."

"Look, I gave that money to you when you needed it. Now I need it."

"You have tons of money sitting in Fidelity, and if you need money that bad, go get some."

"That money is for me and Dad to buy a house in Florida. I can't touch it," he says.

"Ahh, so you're going to bankrupt me because of some fantasy house in Florida?" I feel my blood pressure peaking.

"Send me a hundred a month. That's all I'm asking." He is now pleading.

"Fine, but if I seem thinner when you see me it's because I haven't eaten."

On payday, I send out checks for my bills: truck payment, rent, student loans, utilities, and the three credit cards I've run up to five thousand each. I usually pay double, but have to send the minimum to pay Kev. I have fifty dollars left for gas and food for the next two weeks. So I write Kev an email: *Hey, I really want you to know that I intend on paying you every single penny of the money you loaned me. I appreciate that you gave it to me. But I just can't afford to pay you back right now. I wish I could, but I can't give you what I don't have.*

His response: *Well, I need it. If you don't send me the money, I'll have to take you to court. I already talked to a lawyer and he says a judge will force you on a payment plan.*

"Did you send him a response" Bob asks during our weekly session.

"I did not want to respond until I talked to you," I answer.

"Any idea how you'll respond?"

"None."

"Nothing comes to mind?" he asks in his own inimitable tone, part parental understanding, part indignant query, part condescension like I ought to have a clue at least.

"Several things come to mind. I guess I'll just send him the money."

"Sounds pretty tame, Bryan."

"Yeah, I guess."

"I'm wondering how you're feeling about this."

"Can't you tell?" I ask.

"No, I' can't. You seem cool as a cucumber."

"Do I? I already went through my angry phase," I explain.

"Did you? How so?"

"I don't know. I was just pissed."

"Help me understand what that looks like," Bob says.

"You don't know what anger looks like?" I say, but I realize his point. He has yet to see me screaming pissed.

"I don't know what your anger looks like. See, I think you feel as though your anger is rotten. What you don't realize is that the expression of your anger is what is of utmost importance here, and its expression in this room, so that we can get to its source."

"You want to see it? Fine. I'm fucking outraged! How dare he threaten me with court! Court! After all this family's been through with the fucking legal system, and he's going to haul me into court for a measly three grand?" I have trouble recollecting at what point I rose to my feet, but I'm practically hovering over Bob.

He remains seated, unperturbed. "It looks good on you, Bryan," he says.

"Fuck you. I mean seriously, does he even fathom what it was like for me to wipe our mother's ass and clean her tumors while he was locked up? Fuck him! I did it all. And now he has tens of thousands of dollars sitting in Fidelity because of me and he's going to take me to court for a hundred dollars a month. I mean, am I fucking crazy here or is that the most petty, ungrateful thing you've ever heard?" I storm around the room like a Tasmanian devil.

Bob shrugs. "So tell me, what are you so hurt about?"

"What? Hurt? No. Haven't you been listening? I'm pissed, not hurt!" I say, my chest heaving.

"If anger is a non optional response to pain, then the real question here is: why are you so hurt?"

I collapse as if struck. "I don't know." My voice quivers.

Bob says, "You're safe here."

"He just doesn't get it. He's under their spell. I can't save him. I can't even help him. I let her down. I failed her."

"No, Bryan, she failed you by asking the impossible."

"What do I do?" I ask.

"What do you want from him?"

"I want him to understand what it's been like for me. I want him to get better, to understand that he's completely dependent on my father and grandmother. If he could get away, maybe he'd gain some perspective."

"It doesn't sound like he's going to do that," Bob says.

"No, it doesn't."

"So why do you keep trying?"

"He's my brother."

"Let me ask you this: if a stranger came along and treated you like he's treated you historically, what would you do?" Bob asks.

I ponder his question, but I know the answer. "I'd either fuck him up or run away. Are you suggesting I cut contact with him?"

"I'd never suggest such a thing. But I will point out that, if we based our relationships solely on how people treated us, things would be far different," he explains.

"In that scenario, I'd never talk to any of them."

"Again, I'm not suggesting you have nothing to do with your family. I just question why you go to a well that's dry."

"Habit?"

"I think you suffer from a neurotic loyalty to your family."

"Me too."

That night, after filling up with super unleaded, every press of the gas pedal sets off a tingling in my crotch. It's only after the initial shock of blue lights wears off that I realize I'm doing 75 in a 50.

"What's the hurry this evening?" the state trooper asks after receiving my license and registration.

"No hurry, officer. I just want to get home. It's been a long day," I explain.

Attempts at repositioning my heart from my throat to its origins are thwarted by thoughts of my record glaring on the screen of his onboard computer. Five, ten, fifteen minutes pass. Cars slow to a crawl as they go by. Finally, the officer exits and hands me my documentation back along with a ticket for $250.

"I wrote you a citation. You can pay it or send in the ticket to get a court date to fight it. Slow it down next time," he warns.

"I will, officer."

"By the way, where's your brother, Kevin?" he asks.

Taken aback, I answer, "Probably at my grandmother's. Why?"

"There's a warrant out for him." He answers while shining his flashlight in the rear of the truck.

"For what?" I ask.

"I don't know. That's your grandmother's address, in Saugus?" he asks.

"Yeah."

Driving home, I can't help but feel as if I ratted Kev out. My heart sinks the next morning when Grandma calls to tell me they raided her house and hauled Kev away. I don't mention my run-in with the police, chalking up my getting pulled over to probable cause so the cop could ask me about Kevin. He must've done something to warrant the warrant.

The next day at work, I approach Rich, a state trooper who works out in the gym. I tell him about the ticket in the hopes of pumping him for info about Kev.

"Nothing I can do about that. Sorry," he says.

"Oh, no, I wasn't implying that you could. I was just going to ask if you think I have a chance of fighting it."

"Let me ask you this: were you doing 75?" he asks.

"Of course," I answer. He shrugs.

"Well, thanks for the info."

On the way out, he waves me over and says, "Give me the ticket."

"No, Rich. It's okay. You're right. I deserve it."

"It all depends on whether or not the trooper went back to base or straight home after his shift. If he hasn't handed the ticket in, I can take care of it."

"Thanks man," I say.

An hour later, he calls me at work, "Listen, that's all set. I just told him you're a good kid and just made a mistake. He said you weren't a dick about the ticket and had no problem tossing it."

"Oh my god, Rich. Thank you so much." I gush just a little.

"No problem. So who's this Kevin person to you, your brother?" he asks.

"Yeah, I heard they picked him up."

"They did. I guess he was up on some drug charge. I didn't get a whole lot of details."

"Okay. Thanks again, Rich."

"Kev's sugar plummeted a few weeks ago," Dad explains. "Your grandmother found him on the floor, so she called the paramedics. A police cruiser got there first to assist and found a pile of white powder on a mirror in his room."

"Are you kidding?" I ask.

"I wish I was, son," he answers. "What's strange about it is that they didn't arrest him. They took the powder and issued a citation for him to appear in court, and your brother blew it off so they issued a warrant."

"Doesn't surprise me," I say.

"Why not?"

"Kev's always had a drug problem, even in there. You never noticed?"

"In prison? You sure he was doing it in here?" he asks.

"He used to slide drugs under my door and ask me to hold them, Dad. You really never noticed?"

"God no. Although I'm not sure I'd have known. I'm clueless about that stuff, son," he says, falling back on his tried and true response: ignorance.

"Right. So what's the next step?" I ask.

"He sees a judge next week."

"Let me know what happens."

"Sure thing, son, and can you do me a favor and check in on your grandmother?" he asks.

"No problem."

Jurell is one of my maintenance staff, and yes, I hired him because he's named after Superman's father. He's twenty and reminds me of me at that age, all machismo, hoisting weights he has no business lifting in an attempt to put on size that's never coming. He works hard with supervision, but if let my mind wander, he wanders too and I'll find him in the men's locker room reading the paper. Stuck one Friday night for desk staff, I ask him if he's willing to help out.

During the shift, I ask him to retrieve a bag from a young woman who brought it up to the women's only section. When he comes back, he places the bag under the desk and says, "That girl wants me."

"Really?" I chuckle.

"No doubt in my mind," he answers.

"How can you tell?" I ask.

"Oh, I know," he says, grinning.

"So, ask her out."

"You think I should?" He blushes.

"Totally."

"Isn't there some rule against dating the members?"

"Only if you're a chicken shit."

"I'm no chicken shit. I just don't want to harass her," he says innocently.

"Tell you what. I'll bet you ten bucks I can get a date with her first."

"No offense, but aren't you a little old for her?"

"I got ten bucks right here, just burning a hole in my pocket. You in?" I felt two ways about this situation: if Jurell won, I could stop liking her; and if I won, I won.

Jurell snatched up the ten and ran off to ask her. When he returned, he handed over the ten. "She said no?" I asked.

"Nah, I'm just not ready. But I will ask her tomorrow."

I folded the ten neatly and walked away toward the women-only section, but she wasn't there. Perched above the gym, I spotted her on a stair climber on the main deck. I tried to make it look like I just happened upon her. Forgetting every smooth line I've ever heard, I simply say, "Hi."

"Hey there," she answers.

"You just joined, right?"

"Sure did. Have we met? I have to admit, when I joined I just finished my fourth third-shift in a row so I was a little out of it." She has long dark hair that falls in waves over her shoulders. I almost beg her not to tie it back but think better of it.

"No, I'm Bryan, the general manager."

"I'm Rachel," she says.

She's wearing a tank top with thin spaghetti straps, shorts, and there are two extra elastic ties around her wrist. I can't help but think of a Porsche when I look her over, marveling at the curves. I climb aboard the machine next to hers and notice Jurell watching from the desk, hoping his fuming don't set of the fire alarm.

"What do you do?" I ask.

"I'm a nurse," she answers, toweling off beads of sweat from her forehead.

"Wow, pretty intense."

"It can be."

"What kind of nurse?"

"ICU," she answers.

"Wow, wicked intense."

She chuckles. "Gotta love that accent."

"Accent? Oh, yeah. Sorry. Been here all my life, but I guess the accent kind of stuck," I say.

"Never lived anywhere else?" she asks.

Try to sound worldly, try to sound worldly, is all I can hear in my head. "Oh, yeah. I lived in New Hampshire for a few years, and Florida."

"Oh yeah? Me too. Well, I'm from NH and lived in Sarasota for a few months. I hated it though, so I came back here to go to school." She places her hands on hips that would make a renaissance painter cry. I try not to stare.

"I lived in Clearwater, a nice place to visit but not to live."

I'm ignorant of any signs or symptoms of boredom. She stops the machine and wipes it down, walking over to a mat to stretch.

"So, what's your favorite book?" I ask.

"Why? You like to read?" she asks, sounding surprised.

"Love it."

"What's your favorite book?" she asks.

"I always loved *The Fountainhead* by Ayn Rand. It comes across different every time I read it. I guess maybe because I'm different every time I read it," I say, garnering the scoff of a few jealous meatheads within earshot.

"Oh my, I love that book. What else?"

I try not to watch her stretch but bask in the fact that she's paying more attention to her stretching than me. "I loved *Sophie's World.*"

She ponders the title for a second, then says, "I think I started that book but couldn't get into it. What is it about?'

"It's like a crash course in philosophy."

"Oh yeah. Nah, couldn't do it — too dry for me."

"What about you?" I ask, trying not to get bagged looking down her shirt.

"I'm a total cheese ball. I read these fantasy books by David Eddings. I'm such a geek. I can't believe I'm telling you this."

"Oh please, I'm the king of cheese balls."

There's a pang of disappointment when she gets up, indicating the stretch is over and her workout complete. "Will I see you tomorrow?" I ask.

"Thursday maybe," she replies.

Back at the desk, Jurell renews his resolve after we watch her walk out. "When I see her next, I'm gonna make my move and spend that ten on her."

"Really? Want to make it double or nothing?" I ask.

Simultaneous with his agreement to the new terms, his jaw drops at the sight of Rachel walking in.

"Hey there. I have a question for you," she says before I cut her off.

"Let's go outside." I say. As I walk by Jurell, I whisper, "Close your mouth, you're attracting flies."

I follow her to her car, which is parked haphazardly near the dumpsters. "You said you're free after eight most nights. I'm taking you out for dinner tonight before I go to work at eleven."

"Sure."

"I'll pick you up here."

"See you then."

A moment of pity washes over me as I walk back in, but it vanishes when I remember Jurell's comment about my age.

"Where's my twenty?"

Being so close to a mall has its privileges. I run to a department store to buy a shirt for the date, a blue button-down. Rachel arrives and we decide I should follow her since she'll leave for work afterwards.

"Where are you taking me?" I ask.

"For pho," She replies.

"Pho?"

"Vietnamese soup. Ever been?"

"Can't say that I have. Sounds interesting." I try to sound excited despite my lifelong hatred of ethnic food, including Polish in spite of my origins.

We're seated in a quaint booth not far from tanks that hold exotic fish, probably served with the heads still on, I think, their innards sautéed in other innards.

"You mind if I order for us?" she asks. She's in scrubs and a cotton long sleeve. Her hair is down, prompting me to relax my stringent food aversions.

The waitress takes the order that Rachel points to because she can't pronounce them on the menu. Seconds elapse before crispy spring rolls appear, the mark of efficiency or pre-cooking. Regardless, they're delicious, a testament to the ability of deep-frying to make anything from spring rolls to dog shit tasty.

"So tell me about you," Rachel says, leaning forward.

"What's to tell?" I ask.

"Everything," she replies.

"I run a gym, which is not very exciting. I live in Salem. What else is there?"

"Hmm, for someone with such a worldly taste in books, I figured you had a colorful past."

I stumbled upon *The Fountainhead* in prison, as well as *Sophie's World*, but I wasn't about to open with that. "Oh, my mom was an avid reader," I say.

"Was? So she's no longer with us?" Rachel puts down her roll.

"No. Lung cancer."

"I'm sorry."

"Thanks. She smoked and drank three people's share, and so it wasn't a huge shock. What about you?" I ask, trying to steer the conversation away from me.

"My family is in New Hampshire, not far from Laconia," she says. obviously with the same reticence to delve into family history.

"Are you close to them?"

"Some more than others. What about you?"

I shake my head no.

"I'm sorry. This is a heavy topic for a first date, huh?"

"Not at all. I'm just sitting here wondering how much to lay on you so soon."

"Uh-oh. You're not an axe murderer, are you?" She laughs.

"Hardly. There's no money in it," I reply.

Huge bowls of soup are plopped in front of us, thinly sliced meat floating over thick Asian noodles. We reach for the chop sticks and dig in.

"How long have you been the manager of the gym?" she asks, carefully wiping her mouth after each bite.

"I've been with the company for about four years."

"And before then?"

My default answers stall somewhere between head and mouth until, finally, I just say prison. I figure I've already stumbled. A five-year-old would know I'm hiding something. And the topic has to come up eventually.

"You're kidding, right?" she asks.

"I can only wish."

"For what?"

"My father, brother, and I robbed jewelry stores throughout New England for five years," I say, point blank, no softeners. I just want it out there.

"And how does one get into that?" she asks.

"That is a long story, but some guy ripped my Dad off and so we went after him. After that first success, we just started robbing everyone."

"That's not such a long story," she point out.

"That's the short version."

"We might have to hang out some more so I can get the long one."

"If you're looking for a long one, I'm not your guy."

"You crack me up," she says.

Rachel insists on paying for dinner, then asks me to walk with her to get a coffee before her shift. She sips as we walk back to the cars. "I wish I didn't have to work," she says when we reach out destination.

"Me too."

"Don't try to kiss me. I have coffee breath," she says, shying away.

"What makes you think I want to kiss you?"

Her cell phone rings. She answers while stepping into the doorway of an apartment building. When she steps back out to where I am waiting, she says, "They canceled my shift. Now I have all night. What should we do?"

"I don't know. Want to go for a ride?" I ask.

"Sure."

As we cruise the streets of greater Boston, Rachel thinks out loud. "What is there to do on a Wednesday night?"

"Well, not that I'm inferring anything, but we could go back to my place and watch a movie. No monkey business, I promise."

"Then forget it." She laughs. "That sounds good. Maybe we could stop by my place and pick up some stupid comedies."

We stop at her condo. She pulls movies from the book shelf with abandon. We drive to my place, and we both change into comfy clothes and sit on the couch. Rachel is wearing a duck ensemble, light blue pajama pants with yellow rubber ducks, and a matching white tank top. *Super Troopers* is on, but neither of us is paying much attention. She grills me a little on my past, which I speak of freely for the first time, not feeling ashamed or fearful that anything I say will influence how she feels about me.

Just before dawn, our eyes heavy, we adjourn to my bedroom. I leave on my boxer briefs while she wiggles out of her duck pants to reveal duck underwear.

"If you're trying to tempt me with those wildly sexy undies, it won't work," I joke.

"Well, if these don't get your blood boiling, nothing will."

We snuggle and fall fast asleep. In the morning, I spring out of bed in a panic. "Shit, shit, shit! I was supposed to open the club this morning. Shit, shit, shit!"

Rachel pops up and dresses. "How late are you?" she asks.

"I was supposed to open at five thirty. I'm so dead. The owners hate it when we open late, and this is late."

"Okay, okay. What can I do?" she asks.

"Nothing. Let's just get out of here."

Weaving through traffic, it hits me. "Wait. What day is this?"

"It's Thursday, why?"

She knows by the look on my face. "I have to open tomorrow, not today."

"Oh, good. Then we can have breakfast?" she asks, chuckling over my acute attack of Alzheimer's.

We buy eggs, bacon, and cheese for me to make my famous scramble melt. After breakfast, I drive her to her condo, which is not far from the gym.

"See you tonight?" she asks.

"Sure. I'm closing tonight, so I won't be home until after ten."

"Okay. I'll call you later. There's no way I'll find your place without directions."

Dad calls the next morning. "Hi son, how are things?"

"Not bad. What's going on?"

"I just wanted to let you know your brother is home," he says amidst a flurry of background noise.

"How'd he pull that off?" I ask.

"The judge gave him another chance."

"Lucky him."

"I just wish the kid could catch a break," Dad says.

"This doesn't qualify as a break?" I am snippy and I am sure Dad must hear it.

"It does. Your brother doesn't see it that way, though. He thinks his probation officer is out to get him."

"Listen, Dad. I'm in the middle of something, but I'll leave you with this: Kev is an addict. No one's out to get him except him. Mark my words, he'll use again."

"I just wish I knew how to handle this addiction thing," Dad says.

"I know you don't get it, but it's simple: he can't stop without help."

"Thanks, son. I'll let you go."

"Sorry about that," I tell Rachel. She's sitting on the couch curled up in a blanket.

"It's fine. Was that your dad?" she asks.

"Yeah. My brother is out."

"Why did he go back in?" she asks.

"Apparently he had a hard time with the fact that cocaine is in fact illegal."

"Well, it's not like the law is unclear," she says with a smile.

"Nope. It is pretty straightforward."

"Tell me again why anyone would want to do coke."

"I'm not sure I get it myself," I answer.

"I mean, why wouldn't you just stop?" she asks.

"It's a hard thing to explain."

"My father is an alcoholic.. I've never understood certain things about addiction, like why when that line is crossed, all addicts know how to do is make things worse."

"I wish I could explain it." I say.

"Me too."

I slide in next to her and wrap myself around her. "You know, you haven't slept at your condo since we met," I say.

"I know."

"It's great," I say.

"Good. I'm glad you think so."

Kevin fails a random drug test, prompting the judge to accept probation's recommendation that he return to Concord for the remainder of his probation, two years. Dad is distraught, blaming the judge.

"It's no one's fault but Kevin's," I say.

"They were out to get him from the start," he scoffs.

"Who?"

"His probation officer never gave him a chance."

"That's ridiculous," I argue.

"She was always up his ass."

"You mean she was doing her job? Listen, Kev practically begged to be sent back. I mean, how do you get a second chance after failing the first time and go out and do it again?"

"Just do me a favor and look after your grandmother until I get out," he snaps.

A new painting dons the walls of Bob's office that looks like a forest out of focus, vibrant greens and brown undertones all running together.

"It looks like a forest out of focus. What is it, like an inkblot?" I ask.

Bob shrugs. "It's just a painting I liked, but it's interesting to hear your interpretation. I wonder if you're looking at a forest out of focus."

"Feels like it."

Bob nods. "Tell me."

"I don't think I can talk to them anymore," I say.

"Your family."

"There's nothing for me there but misery."

"A tough choice."

"The right one?" I ask.

Bob shrugs again, somberly adding, "My brother called me a few years ago to tell me my mother was in the hospital. I was torn as to whether or not to visit her, but I went. She was dying, same as your mother, so I sat with her, held her hand, and told her I forgave her. Then I walked out."

"And?" I ask.

Bob shrugs again.

"You don't even talk to your brother?" I ask.

"I base my relationships on treatment. He never treated me very well, or I him, for that matter, so why maintain that kind of relationship. We were amicable at the funeral, but I haven't talked to him since."

"How do you do it without feeling guilty?" I ask.

"I remind myself that guilt in the absence of a crime is neurotic, and I remind myself that, when the conveyor belt ceases to give up goodies and starts rolling out bad treatment, it's hard to get that conveyor belt to stop."

"It's just really hard. I always thought that hell would make us stronger. I don't get how we ended up here."

"What don't you get?" Bob asks.

"Why we're so different, Kevin and me," I say.

"How do you understand why you're here and he's there?"

"You mean therapy? We were both dragged to therapy as kids. So what makes me so different?" I ask.

"At some point you saw the value. He didn't."

"Mom did that for me."

"How so?" Bob asks.

"I went because it made her happy," I admit.

"And in doing so, she did you a great service, a service your brother chooses to ignore."

"I think my brother took Mom and Dad's divorce much harder than I did."

"And you said he was always in trouble?" Bob asks.

"We both were in trouble, but him more than me."

"And how did your parents deal with him?"

"I always knew when he got into trouble because Dad's car would be in the driveway when I got home from school."

"Your mother called him?"

"Always."

"So he got into trouble because she would summon your father and reunite them under a common cause. And how did you cope when things like that were going on?"

I sit and stew before answering. "When I wasn't actively trying to get sick, I hid. A beating could come from any direction at any time, and so I withdrew."

"And your brother went out of his way just to catch a glimpse of what life was like in his earliest memories, which explains his refusal to self actualize through therapy."

"So in some ways, your painting seems clearer to me than it would to him."

Bob shrugs and smiles.

At work I reach a group exercise class. I work the class harder than usual: push-ups, squats, and burpies with no rest. I feed off the energy exuding from the class members and push harder. Sweat pours from everyone, and they are parched because I've given them no chance to drink. Deb, a health teacher at a suburban high school, approaches me after class.

"Hard class. Do you hate us?" she asks jokingly.

"Nope. I love you all, and that's why that hurt me more than it hurt you," I answer.

"Listen. I was wondering of you'd be interested in coming to the high school to talk to my health classes about fitness?"

"I'd love to. When?"

"I'll have to look at the curriculum, but in the next few weeks," she says, wiping sweat off her brow.

"Do you need speakers on any other topics?" I ask.

"Like what?"

"Well, I have an Associate's in substance abuse counseling and a Bachelor's in psychology." I pause for a moment and then add, "And I've been in recovery for a few years."

She leans in close. "I can't tell you how hard it is to find a person to discuss addiction that isn't, well, you know?"

"A toothless basket case?" I ask.

"The last guy was a nightmare. The kids just couldn't relate."

"I'll do my best then."

Lexington High is in the quintessential upscale suburb: sprawling mansions, massive acreages, a town center. It all amounts to elegantly engineered hominess with a hint of convenience. The school looks more like a university, with separate buildings according to discipline. The health building flanks the science building. Deb's office is on the second floor.

I enlisted Rachel and her sister to help dress me for the occasion. We settled on an Abercrombie sweatshirt, faded jeans, and my brown shoes. I'll speak to every junior and senior in the school. Racing over the finer points of my story, I sit in the class, watching students roll in. The Smarties sit up front, Moderates in the middle, Troubles in back. The Moderates act as go-betweens for the Troubles should one require a Smarty's assistance. I was a Trouble.

Deb covers the particulars she'd like me to cover: coping skills, basic education, signs and symptoms. When she introduces me, she lists accolades I'm not sure I possess. Random heads turn in my direction, assessing me. Once unleashed, my nervousness fades and I meld into my story.

The students' eyes gloss over at first. The Troubles busy themselves with texts, doodles, and neglected homework due next period. When I reach the first robbery, I grab all their attention and every student's eyes are on me. I draw a map on the board of where my brother and I stood in relation to the house. The Troubles lean forward so as not to miss even the slightest inflection.

Not expecting much by way of questions, I leave five minutes for the students to ask what they want to know, but nearly every hand goes up.

"Where is your dad now?" the front row asks.

"What is prison like?" the middle joins in.

"Did you kill anyone," comes from the back.

The bell rings. Students shake my hand on the way out. A sheepish girl with a mouth full of metal asks if I'll sign her notebook. Back in the teachers' lounge, I'm praised for my ability to grab their attention. Deb sits quiet and waits.

"I had no idea your story was so intense," she says. She adds, "I like the parts about the coping skills, and you did a great job showing them the consequences of your actions."

"And?" I ask, knowing a detailed critique is coming.

"Try not to glorify the robberies. Not that you did, but we have some kids who might sit there and listen to you, thinking, 'He got into all that trouble and he's okay now,'" Deb says while the other teachers nod.

As the day wears on, the content of my story spreads throughout the campus and Troubles begin to move into the front row for the next show. Some from the previous presentation show up to hear it again.

Consequences

After six years of working for Gold's, I decide to leave. I want to return to counseling addicts, a fire my trip to Lexington rekindles. Unfortunately, I get turned down for every job I apply for, two of which were particularly disappointing: one with a treatment center for troubled youth and the other managing a student health center at a college. For each I filled out a CORI. The treatment center sends me a form letter telling me they're unable to hire me at this time. The college sends a thank you card stating they went with another candidate.

It feels like I am sinking, as if a switch has been flicked and I am now standing in the dark after finally finding the damned light. I suffer from more than a loss of motivation. My depression seals me off so that no one can reach, touch, or console me. I stop going to therapy. I contact lawyers and inquire about sealing my criminal record. They tell me it can't be sealed until 2017, fifteen years after the last day of probation. I return to fitness as a personal trainer. They never do background checks.

A few days later I get a letter from Dad, the first in over a year. I set the letter on the coffee table and study it. It's thin. The post mark proves it's recent, and there's no mistaking the penmanship. I open it and read:

Dear Bryan,

It's been a long time since I've heard from you. It's clear from your refusal to contact us that you've chosen to isolate yourself from your family. If this is your decision then this will be the last letter you receive. If you'd like to be a part of this family, you can start by contacting you grandmother. She turns 92 this month, and the least you can do is wish her happy birthday.

I'd really like to have a relationship with you when I get out. That I'll leave up to you. If I don't hear from you, I'll consider that your answer.

Dad

I read it a few times, growing angrier by the second. I grab my computer and write back:

Dear Dad,

It was a shock to hear from you. I'm glad you're well and will be getting out soon. As for my relationship with Kev, I had hoped you'd stay out of it. Seeing as though you have only heard his side, I'll tell you that his threat to take me to court was more than I was willing to put up with. As for Grandma, I suspect she's on his side since my phone hasn't rung either.

As for our relationship, I'll say this: what relationship?

Dad's release date comes and goes, and I have no way of knowing if he received my letter. After work one day, I drive to Grandma's and park down the street and stare at the house, hoping to catch a glimpse.

A week later, Dad calls and I agree to meet him for lunch. He pulls up in a brand new Nissan Pathfinder. He hasn't aged a day. I remain seated to avoid and physical contact.

"Hi there, son," he says, sitting down gingerly, as if in pain.

"I see the knees are still bothering you," I say.

"Yeah. I have good days and, unfortunately, bad days. How are you?" he asks.

"Good. How does it feel?" I ask.

"Being out? It's an adjustment, I'll tell you that."

"I see you're traveling in style," I say, gesturing toward the truck.

"Man's gotta get around," he jokes. "How's your truck doing?"

"I traded it in for a Volkswagen Golf because the gas prices were killing me."

"I can relate. Mine rides like a dream, but I think I get two miles to the gallon."

"No doubt."

"It's good to see you, son. It's been a long time."

"So what are you going to do now that you're out?"

"Wait for your brother to wrap up. He's in Concord and will probably stay there. Then, I am off to Florida, I guess. How about you?" he asks.

"I'm in a serious relationship and working, and that's about it."

"I'd love to meet her," he says.

"You'll have to come to dinner sometime," I say.

"I'd love to, son."

We eat and engage in small talk. There's no talk of the letter, his or mine. After our meal, he hugs me and says he'll be in touch.

Rachel slaves over a hot stove while I stare out the window. "Is he here yet?" she asks.

"Not yet."

"Babe, try to relax. It'll be fine."

"I'm so nervous and I don't know why."

"It is understandable," she says. "You have not spent any time with him for a long while."

When he arrives, Rachel greets him as if she's know him for years, hugging him and offering a glass of wine.

"I'd love one," he says, sitting on the couch.

Over dinner, Rachel keeps the conversation light, never letting his glass stay empty. Talk turns to the robberies. Rachel asks, "Is it hard to adjust to being out?"

"It was at first, but now I'm used to it," Dad admits.

"You did twelve years, right? What was that like?" she asks.

"Oh, I had it better than most," he answers. "I worked in the kitchen with a guy that collected for the mob and ended up killing someone. He was a great cook. After we fed the population, he'd whip us up a meal. Boy did I eat. That's why I never needed canteen money. I ate like a king."

I scoff, "And lived in an air-conditioned dorm with the rest of the workers."

"What can I say? It's good to have connections." Dad smirks.

"How did you guys get away with not seriously hurting anyone?" Rachel asks.

"Hon, we robbed a guy twice," I blurt out. "We did not cave anyone's skull in, but we took all this guy had."

"Really?" she asks.

"We bankrupted him. He had to move back to Israel," I answer.

She turns to Dad. "And you don't feel bad about that?"

Straight faced, he says, "He ripped me off. He deserved it."

"What will you do now?" Rachel asks, obviously changing the subject.

"Oh, I'm not really sure. I can't work fulltime or they'll decrease my social security. At some point, I'll draw off the interest of my retirement fund, which by the way, I need to talk to you about," he says to me.

"Okay," I reply.

"Well, when you transferred my money to Fidelity, I had you and your brother as equal recipients of the money upon my death. I've recently changed that. Your brother is going to get a higher percentage."

I see Rachel squirm in my peripheral vision. I am unaffected by his words, mostly because things have been uneven between my brother and me and our dad since we were born. Why should Dad's death be any different?

"Why?" I ask, more to make him say something than because I care.

"I imagine your brother is going to need extra care because of his diabetes," he answers.

"Of course," I say, waving off Rachel's rebuttal.

Dad swills wine and swishes it around his mouth before gulping it down. "I do make a little extra here and there selling jewelry," he says.

"What?" Rachel and I say simultaneously.

"I have a friend who owns a store, nothing big."

"Dad, I'm not going back to prison," I joke.

"Neither am I, son."

Where Are They Now?

It's my sixth straight year at Lexington, and Deb tells me that, when they tally the vote for the year's most memorable speaker, I win almost unanimously. I note that the faces change but the configuration stays the same: Smarties up front and Troubles in the back. The questions vary, but almost every class asks, "Where's your dad now?"

"He lives with my 94 year-old grandmother and my brother."

"Do you still see him?"

"Occasionally. I've accepted the fact that he'll never be the ideal dad, and I have tried to accept him for what he is: self-absorbed and mostly checked out when it comes to any wrongs he has committed in his life. To his credit, I think he tries really hard to be in my life."

"What about your brother?"

"We haven't spoken in nine years."

"Do you ever feel tempted to use drugs again?"

"I learned early on in my recovery to think the drink through. So now, if I want to use, I can look through to the consequences and that pretty much ends any cravings."

One gets shot at me from the back: "What's it like in prison?"

"If you want to know what it's like, you can do an experiment. Go home and clear anything fun or that could be used as a weapon from your bathroom and sit in the tub for three years. As if that isn't bad enough, have a guard come by and strip search you regularly. Oh, I almost forgot: you're not alone in prison, so in your little experiment, find a stranger to throw in the mix for a cellmate, one who may or may not be a sex offender."

In the absence of any hope that they'll change the CORI laws and I'll go back to counseling addicts, I stay in fitness and travel to schools when my schedule permits.

There are times that I'm perplexed as to what prompted me to change and to seek out reasons for why I struggled so hard in life. I attribute a lot of it to my mother's insistence that we attend therapy as kids. Kev's refusal to lay credence to the power of insight leads me to believe that somewhere along the way, I heard something he didn't.

We both survived childhood, braved addiction, and made it through prison. But I surpassed my brother, whose refusal to seek out the roots of his dysfunction keeps him in a holding pattern, while I try to come up with reasons why I ended up where I did, and try to figure out how to never end up there again.

Some attribute the changes I've made to intelligence; others say it's because I'm more self- aware. Me, I think it merely lies in the realization that some change is inevitable, and some change is optional.

THE BOSTON HERALD, FRIDAY, SEPTEMBER 29, 1995

AG and MBTA differ on plan to fight bigotry

By LAURA BROWN

Transportation Secretary James J. Kerasiotes and Attorney General Scott Harshbarger each said yesterday they hoped to hammer out a plan to deal with discrimination and harassment at the MBTA.

But the two appeared to be miles apart on finding a way to finalize the deal.

"There's been an investigation going on for the past year, and we found serious systemic problems with sexual harassment, discrimination and retaliation," Harshbarger said.

"It's time for an agreement in writing that's enforceable and will deal with past discrimination and implement remedies," he added. "We really need a court-approved plan."

Harshbarger has argued that any agreement short of a court-ordered plan could be derailed by a complaint from one of the MBTA's 27 unions.

MBTA General Manager Patrick J. Moynihan yesterday countered that the deal Harshbarger wants is "overreaching and unnecessary."

"A consent decree or judicial enforcement sends a message to our employees we're being compelled to do something we wouldn't otherwise do, and that's just not the case," Moynihan said.

He claimed that every part of a proposed agreement with the Attorney General's office addresses something that T officials have already done or intend to do.

According to Assistant Attorney General Richard Cole, the T's remaining "barriers" in dealing with the problems that have resulted in 135 pending cases include severe understaffing in departments that deal with complaints and the lack of any tra-lized system to collect complaint data.

"The clock is ticking and it's clear this is only a very short time frame," Cole added, saying the next likely step may be a lawsuit against the T.

Meanwhile, workers who have filed discrimination complaints against the T say they feel vindicated.

"The attorney general's position shows this group is not just disgruntled and out-of-line — that we have some legitimate concerns," said Craig Dias, a spokesman for a group called Concerned Minority Employees.

Agencies can't be trusted to fight racism on their own

LEONARD GREENE

She knew where the phone call came from, but she couldn't tell who placed it. Her caller identification box gave her a number, but it wouldn't give her a name.

Still, it was enough to know that the lewd comments coming through her phone were coming from her place of employment. For months, male co-workers had been pelting her with sexist jokes and filthy language.

Now they were calling her at home.

For more than a year, officials have been investigating sexual and racial harassment complaints at the MBTA, including the phone call to the worker with the ID box.

"The harassment has gotten more anonymous," said Cathy Ziehl, director of the state attorney general's employment discrimination project. "It's brazen but it's also cowardly because the person is not identified."

What was once overt and blatant employee harassment has become covert and subtle retaliation. The punishment for formal complaints ranges from miserable work assignments to threatening phone calls at home.

The situation at the Massachusetts Bay Transportation Authority has gotten so bad and is so widespread that Attorney General Scott Harshbarger has considered filing civil rights charges unless MBTA officials agree to a settlement that would include court supervision.

Harshbarger was expecting action on an agreement earlier this week, but has yet to get anyone's signature on a legal document.

The agreement did not even come up during a public meeting Wednesday of the MBTA board of directors. Only after a private meeting was General Manager Patrick Moynihan directed to form a task force to deal with racial issues.

"We're very disappointed," said Assistant Attorney General Richard Cole. "For a year, we've had nine people engaged in an investigation and we kept it quiet. We really think it's regrettable that apparently the board has not agreed to enter into this agreement in principle."

The harassment described in complaints and by workers comes straight from the racist and chauvinist handbooks: Big-lipped caricatures of black men in locker rooms; physical confrontations with women in hallways.

"The calls at home are a new twist, but they're in the handbook, too.

"It's not just in one area," said Craig Dias, who founded the Concerned Minority Employees group two years ago to address the situation.

"It's throughout the system."

Dias filed a complaint of his own after he said a co-worker attacked him with a shovel. The co-worker, Dias said, had offered him the shovel, telling him to "dig like my people on the plantation."

Che Chung Chi, a Chinese immigrant from Hong Kong, has three discrimination cases pending against the MBTA. The former inspector said he was demoted after filing his complaint and said he was never given any valid reasons.

"Because I speak with an accent, they discriminated against me," he said. "And when I filed a complaint they retaliated against me."

Cole said such complaints have been difficult for the MBTA to examine internally. He said the agency does not have enough investigators or a centralized data collection system to identify patterns of abuse.

"There's no one who is focusing on the broad-based problems," Cole said. "You have to have a credible internal investigative procedure."

Moynihan agrees. In fact, he agrees with all the provisions of the attorney general's settlement, except one — the consent decree.

"When you enter into those agreements, it sends a message that you're being compelled to do something that you otherwise wouldn't do," Moynihan said. "That is not the case."

Those of us on the receiving end of discrimination know that no effective remedy to bigotry and sexism has ever come without court supervision.

If agencies such as the MBTA or the School Department could be trusted to root out discrimination, there would never have been these kinds of problems in the first place.

In this fight against discrimination, we must learn to trust no one. No handshakes, no promises, no commitments, no gods. Without court supervision, an agency's word is worthless.

Their agreement and a token will get you on the subway.

Mastermind of father-son jewel heist team jailed

By SIMON PRISTEL

A college-educated Nashua, N.H., electronics salesman who pulled a series of elaborate jewelry heists across the state with the help of his two sons to pay for their college tuition was jailed yesterday.

"This concludes a bizarre series of crimes that I am still unable to fully understand," Dedham Superior Court Judge Julian Houston said after sentencing John Sobolewski to 12 years.

"It is really quite extraordinary and very, very sad."

Sobolewski, 54 — the mastermind of the robbery team that netted nearly $2 million over several years — yesterday changed his plea from not guilty to guilty on armed robbery, conspiracy to commit armed robbery and carjacking charges.

His son, Kevin, 28, is already serving an 8-year jail sentence, while his other son, Brian, 25, is serving 2½ years behind bars. Another man, William Lawson is serving a 7- to 10-year term.

Assistant Attorney General Howard Wise told the court that in one scam in October 1993 Sobolewski posed as a legitimate jewel buyer. But when the Harwick jewelry shop worker, Nell Waters, $6, showed him the jewels, one of Sobolewski's sons burst in with a gun.

As the son sat on Waters with the gun pointed at his face and threatening to kill him, the elder Sobolewski made off with $200,000 worth of uninsured jewels, none of which were ever recovered.

In another incident in Burlington in June 1992, the Sobolewski gang robbed a man and then threatened to kill his family if he didn't tell police black men were to blame.

The 38-year-old victim became very depressed and died of a heart attack 18 months later. The man's wife still lives in fear of the Sobolewski family, authorities said.

Sobolewski showed no emotion as he was sentenced and refused to speak up for himself, but his mother, Theresa, did not stop sobbing.

Outside the court Sobolewski's attorney, Ray O'Hara, said his client committed the crimes in part to help pay for college tuition for his sons, both of whom were either crack addicts or reformed addicts, he said.

"We all have to live with our choices in this world," O'Hara told Sobolewski.

"He is going to live with it for a while."

SENTENCED: John Sobolewski pleads guilty in court yesterday to armed robbery, conspiracy to commit armed robbery and carjacking. He was sentenced to 12 years in prison. — Staff photo by George Rizer

THE BOSTON GLOBE • FRIDAY, MARCH 17, 1995

Visitation center's data denied to father

CAMBRIDGE – A Middlesex probate judge yesterday rescinded an earlier order and ruled that an Algerian national, who may visit his son only in a supervised setting, may not learn the identities of staff members of the Brockton visitation center where he visits with his son.

Ralph Boudfia is trying to earn the right to unsupervised meetings with his son, Ahmed. His attorney, Lawrence Glick, had argued to Judge Nancy Gould that he needs the names and addresses of staff members and volunteers to pursue his case.

Women who fear meeting the fathers of their children alone bring their children to the visiting center when they are under order to allow the fathers to visit them.

Patricia Kelliher, the center's director, has maintained that keeping personnel data confidential is vital to the center's operation. Her attorney, Robert Clark, yesterday persuaded Gould to reverse her order of Jan. 11 that would have given Glick access to the records.

However, Jane Podolski, attorney for the child's mother, Susan Bondfia, failed to persuade Gould to overturn the part of her Jan. 11 order that requires the mother to give the father the child's medical records.

Ex-mental health care executives plead guilty to Medicaid fraud

By Judy Rakowsky
GLOBE STAFF

Three former mental health care executives pleaded guilty yesterday in US District Court in Springfield to defrauding the federal government, six states and the local government of Washington, D.C. of up to $2.5 million in Medicaid funds intended for services to mentally retarded clients.

L. Thomas Culpeppen, 62, of Wilbraham, Paul Culpeppen, 39, of Sumter, Clint, and Louis Calhoun, 49, of Amherst, pleaded guilty to mail fraud, wire fraud and conspiracy before US District Judge Michael Ponsor.

The men developed an elaborate scheme that involved fictitious companies and billing to inflate the costs, said US Attorney Donald K. Stern.

"They stole from the mental health care system under the fully

gines of bulging others," Stern said. The three men waived indictment and admitted to the charges.

Previously, Albert J. Diaz, 62, of Loefins, and Eugene J. Kaminski of Belchertown, who at one time headed the Center for Residential Change in Springfield, pleaded guilty to similar charges and cooperated with the federal probe.

Eight nonprofit agencies were defrauded of funds through reliance of false invoices, inflated payments and kickbacks to the principals of Executive Management Associates, a for-profit corporation, prosecutors said. EMA generated profits through a management contract of the nonprofit companies.

The nonprofit companies were billed for furniture and equipment, with extra costs kickbacks for resale by companies that existed only as a device to inflate costs, according to court documents.

The scheme involved an elaborate system of service-providing agencies and reams of paperwork that covered up expenditures such as a golf membership course for which the nonprofit companies were billed $5,000 for training costs, the documents said.

The case grew out of a 1991 whistleblower action that identified billing irregularities and prompted an extensive review of the Center for Residential Change by state Auditor A. Joseph DeNucci.

"The system really worked well in this case," said Glenn Briere, spokesman for DeNucci, who released the audit to the public at the conclusion of the cases proceeding in Springfield.

The investigation was developed by a task force of law enforcement officers and auditors from the inspector general's office of the US Department of Health and Human Services.

Suspect in jewel robberies arrested in N.H.

A New Hampshire man has been arrested and charged with masterminding seven armed robberies in Massachusetts and Rhode Island since July 1993 that netted about $2.5 million worth of jewels, authorities said yesterday.

John P. Bobelewski, 52, was arrested Wednesday after he tried to flee a police dishpand near the Nashua home, officials said. He was charged with an interstate theft and apprehended near the Massachusetts border.

According to Massachusetts Attorney General Scott Harshbarger, Bobelewski is a suspect in the robbery of stores or jewelry salesmen in Burlington, Chicopee, Harwich, Littleton, Methuen and Weymouth, Mass., and Warwick, R.I.

He was also wanted in a 1994 charge of attempted robbery of a New Hampshire jewelry salesman. He is being held on that charge until Massachusetts completes extradition proceedings, authorities said.

Massachusetts State Trooper Elizabeth Burke, who is assigned to the attorney general's office, noted a pattern among the robberies, authorities said.

According to Harshbarger's office, Burke found that in all of the robberies, the victim had had a row dealings with a well-dressed, articulate man who claimed to work in the jewelry industry. Also, the robberies took place when a meeting had been scheduled and a jewel prepared for showing, officials said.

A burglary and apprehended of ROJAM is jewelry believed to have been stolen during at least one of the armed robberies, was recovered in the car Bobelewski was driving, authorities said.

Harshbarger's office said Bobelewski allegedly led a ring of three to five accomplices, and additional arrests are expected.

MAR 17 1995

270

Visitation center's data denied to father

CAMBRIDGE - A Middlesex probate judge yesterday rescinded an earlier order and ruled that an Algerian national, who may visit his son only in a supervised setting, may not learn the identities of staff members of the Brockton visitation center where he visits with his son.

Rabah Boudiaf is trying to earn the right to unsupervised meetings with his son, Ahmed. His attorney, Lawrence Glick, had argued to Judge Nancy Gould that he needs the names and addresses of staff members and volunteers to pursue his case.

Women who fear meeting the fathers of their children alone bring their children to the visiting center when they are under order to allow the fathers to visit them.

Patricia Kelliher, the center's director, has maintained that keeping personnel data confidential is vital to the center's operation. Her attorney, Robert Clark, yesterday persuaded Gould to reverse her order of Jan. 11 that would have given Glick access to the records.

However, Jane Podolski, attorney for the child's mother, Senora Boudiaf, failed to persuade Gould to overturn the part of her Jan. 11 order that requires the mother to give the father the child's medical records.

Ex-mental health care executives plead guilty to Medicaid fraud

By Judy Rakowsky
GLOBE STAFF

Three former mental health care executives pleaded guilty yesterday in US District Court in Springfield to defrauding the federal government, six states and the local government of Washington D.C. of up to $2.5 million in Medicaid funds intended for services to mentally retarded clients.

C. Thomas Campagna, 51, of Wilbraham, Paul Campagna, 39, of Somers, Conn., and Louis Gallinaro, 49, of Amherst, pleaded guilty to mail fraud, wire fraud and conspiracy before US District Judge Michael Ponsor.

The men developed an elaborate scheme that involved fictitious companies and billing to cover the thefts, said US Attorney Donald K. Stern. "They stole from the mental health care system under the lofty guise of helping others," Stern said. The three men waived indictment and admitted to the charges.

Previously, Albert J. Dias, 42, of Ludlow, and Eugene J. Karmelek of Belchertown, who at one time headed the Center for Humanistic Change in Springfield, pleaded guilty to similar charges and cooperated with the federal probe.

Eight nonprofit agencies were defrauded of funds through schemes of false invoices, inflated payments and kickbacks to the principals of Executive Management Associates, a for-profit corporation, prosecutors said. EMA generated profits through a management contract of the nonprofit companies.

The nonprofit companies were billed for furniture and equipment, with extra costs tacked on for resale by companies that existed only as a device to inflate costs, according to court documents.

The scheme involved an alphabet of service-providing agencies and reams of paperwork that covered up expenditures such as a golf instruction course for which the nonprofit companies were billed $5,000 for training costs, the documents said.

The case grew out of a 1991 Globe Spotlight series that identified billing irregularities and prompted an extensive review of the Center for Humanistic Change by state Auditor A. Joseph DeNucci.

"The system really worked well in this case," said Glenn Briere, spokesman for DeNucci, who released the audit to the public at the conclusion of the court proceeding in Springfield.

The investigation was developed by a task force of law enforcement officers and auditors from the inspector general's office of the US Department of Health and Human Services.

Suspect in jewel robberies arrested in N.H.

A New Hampshire man has been arrested and charged with masterminding seven armed robberies in Massachusetts and Rhode Island since July 1993 that netted about $2.5 million worth of jewels, authorities said yesterday.

John F. Sobolewski, 52, was arrested Wednesday after he tried to flee a police stakeout near his Nashua home, officials said. He was chased south on Interstate 93 and apprehended near the Massachusetts border.

According to Massachusetts Attorney General Scott Harshbarger, Sobolewski is a suspect in the rob-

bery of stores or jewelry salesmen in Burlington, Chicopee, Harwich, Littleton, Methuen and Weymouth, Mass., and Warwick, R.I.

He was also wanted on a 1991 charge of attempted robbery of a New Hampshire jewelry salesman. He is being held on that charge until Massachusetts completes extradition proceedings, authorities said.

Massachusetts State Trooper Elizabeth Burke, who is assigned to the attorney general's office, noticed a pattern among the holdups, authorities said.

According to Harshbarger's office, Burke found that in all of the

robberies, the victims had had extensive dealings with a well-dressed, articulate man who claimed to work in the jewelry industry. Also, the robberies took place when a meeting had been scheduled and jewelry prepared for showing, officials said.

A handgun and approximately $250,000 in jewelry were recovered in the car Sobolewski was driving, authorities said.

Harshbarger's office said Sobolewski allegedly led a ring of three to five accomplices, and additional arrests are expected.

THE BOSTON GLOBE ● FRIDAY, DECEMBER 29, 1995

overage may pay off this year

ke
et

———

uch a
rough
ng up
cities,
ggling
y-seay-
{
ne in-
muni-
cified
lowly
g out
/inter

setts
y for
kton.
e re-
last

: you
itrick
City
e lost
-otect
: ex-

-utive
icipal
il in-
o say
. will
pur-

ictice
:auge
that
into
said
blan-
nean
nket-

orld-
City
said
oular
nited
erta,

ousi-
ities
r. In

the long term we expect to make money on this, but not hand over fist. We see it as way to project cost into future for small fee."

Winter 1995-96 may be one of those years when the insurance pays off.

For example, this year Massport purchased a snow removal policy that will kick in after 44 inches of snow falls this season, said Massport Director Stephen Tocco.

Given that nearly 30 inches have fallen at Logan so far this year, the chances are good that Massport made the right move, he said.

"We couldn't have picked a better year to try this," Tocco said. "This is the most snow we've ever had this early."

In the winter of 1993-94, when 96.3 inches of snow fell at Logan, the cost of snow removal was more than $2.5 million, said Thomas J. Kinton Jr., director of aviation at Logan.

Massport purchased its policy for $300,000. It carries a $100,000 deductible, applicable when the first claim is filed. If snow accumulation exceeds 44 inches Massport will be paid $50,000 per inch for up to 40 inches, potentially saving the agency as much as $1.6 million in a given year.

"It looks like it might work this year," Kinton said. "People might criticize this if we only had 14 inches of snow, but the point is you have it there and it levels out the cost from year to year."

Robert Smith, Brockton's chief financial officer, said the policy the city purchased covers storms of 4.5 or more inches, starting with the fifth storm.

Brockton will receive $50,000 for each storm up to $500,000 or ten storms. The policy cost the city $17,500.

"We all decided that insurance is a crap-shoot at best but we decided, 'why not be prudent and wise and think ahead,'" said Smith. "You plan for the worst and hope for the best."

Northampton's policy cost $3,000 and will pay $4,500 per inch for anything over 50 inches of snow, said Goggins. City records indicate that six out of every 25 years the city gets enough snow to collect from the policy.

Ron Wardynski takes a spill yesterday while sledding in a plastic recycling bin at Farragut Park in South Boston.

GLOBE STAFF PHOTO / BILL GREENE

Taking a chance on winter

During the record-setting winter of 1993-94, removing the season's eight feet of snow at Logan International Airport cost Massport $2.5 million. For the first time, Massport bought snow insurance this year, at a cost of $300,000. The policy will pay $50,000 per inch if the airport gets more than 44 inches of snow, up to 40 additional inches.

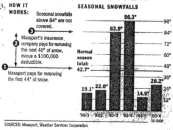

HOW IT WORKS:

3 — Seasonal snowfalls above 84" are not covered.

2 — Massport's insurance company pays for removing the next 40" of snow, minus a $100,000 deductible.

1 — Massport pays for removing the first 44" of snow.

SEASONAL SNOWFALLS

96.3"		96"
83.9"		84"
		72"
Normal season total: 42.7"		60"
		48"
	28.2" 36"	
19.1" 22.0"	14.9" 24"	
		12"

'90/1 '91/2 '92/3 '93/4 '94/5 '95/6 to date

SOURCES: Massport, Weather Services Corporation

GLOBE STAFF GRAPHIC

Beverly also renewed its snow removal policy despite filing no claims last year.

"Last year we didn't cash in but this year we might collect on it," said Peter Seamans, administrative aide to Mayor William F. Scanlon. "With this policy we avoid having that one year of a budget buster."

In Boston the idea has not

sparked much interest, however.

Joseph Cassazza, city public works director, said that officials did take a quick look at the concept several years ago, but were not convinced of its value.

"I remember the concept coming up," Cassaza said. "We certainly didn't disregard it but we decided not to pursue it."

Holyoke's ex-mayor and successor feud

(anbhara) to fashion an insult ha-

New England News Briefs

Two arrested for 1992 robbery

Two men were arrested yesterday in connection with the 1992 armed robbery of $350,000 from a Burlington jeweler, according to the office of state Attorney General Scott Harshbarger. The attorney general said William Lawson, 38, of Upton, and Brian Sobolewski, 25, of Nashua, were indicted by a Middlesex grand jury on charges that included armed robbery and larceny over $250. Lawson pleaded not guilty to the charges, and was ordered held on $50,000 cash bail. Sobolewski is in custody pending arraignment. Sobolewski's father, John, 52, and his brother, Kevin, 27, are also being held in connection with the robbery.

Ex-state cashier charged in theft

BOSTON – A former state Department of Public Safety cashier has been indicted on charges she stole up to $20,000 from the department. Betty Lee Wing, 49, of Newton, allegedly stole money orders, bank checks and treasurer's checks used to pay for state-issued licenses for construction and other trades. Wing, who worked for the department from 1978 until six months ago, was to be charged with larceny and publishing false reports. (AP)

Lowell man faces kidnap charge

A Lowell man was indicted by a federal grand jury yesterday on carjacking and kidnapping charges in connection with the Dec. 10 abduction of a woman from Lowell to New Hampshire, said US Attorney Donald K. Stern. The indictment of Paul E. Lowe, 26, which included a charge of using a firearm during a crime of violence, offered no details of the incident. The FBI, Middlesex District Attorney's office, Lowell police and US Attorney's office refused comment, citing concern for the victim. US Magistrate Judge Robert Collings ordered Lowe held without bail until a detention hearing next week.

Motorcycle driver to be resentenced

PORTLAND, Maine - Archdiocese

Printed in Great Britain
by Amazon

54358205R00155